Carol Field Dahlstrom

Christmas
in the
Nick of
Time

750

Easy-to-Make ideas for crafting, cookie-baking,
gift-giving, decorating, and memory-making

Carol Field Dahlstrom, Inc.
Brave Ink Press
Ankeny, Iowa

Author and Editor
Carol Field Dahlstrom

Book Design
Lyne Neymeyer

Photography: Pete Krumhardt, Andy Lyons, Dean Tanner–Primary Image
Copy Editing: Janet Figg, Jill Philby
Proofreading: Elizabeth Dahlstrom, Judy Bailey
Food Artist: Jennifer Peterson
Props and Location: Roger Dahlstrom
Technical Assistant: Judy Bailey
How-to Illustrations: Kristen Krumhardt
Recipe Development and Testing: Elizabeth Dahlstrom, Ardith Field,
    Barbara Hoover, Jennifer Peterson

Special thanks to these people for helping to make some of the items in the book:
Donna Chesnut, Kristin Detrick, Ardith Field, Barbara Hoover,
    Janet Petersma, Jennifer Peterson, Barbara Sestok, Ann E. Smith, Jan Temeyer

ISBN 978-09768446-7-9
Library of Congress Control Number: 2008904202
Copyright © Carol Field Dahlstrom, Inc. 2008

Separations: Integrity Printing, Des Moines, Iowa
Printed in the United States of America
First Edition

ABOUT THE AUTHOR

Carol Field Dahlstrom has produced over 90 best-selling crafts, food, decorating, children's, and
holiday books for Better Homes and Gardens®, Bookspan®, and her own publishing company,
Brave Ink Press. She has made numerous television, radio, and speaking appearances, sharing her
books and encouraging simple and productive ways to spend family time together. Her creative
vision and experience make her books fun as well as informative. She lives with her family in the
country near Des Moines, Iowa, where she writes and designs from her studio.

Carol Field Dahlstrom, Inc. and Brave Ink Press strive to provide high quality products and information that will make your
life happier and more beautiful. Please write or e-mail us with your comments, questions, and suggestions, or to inquire
about purchasing books, at braveink@aol.com or Brave Ink Press, P.O. Box 663, Ankeny, Iowa 50021.

Visit us at **www.braveink.com** to see upcoming books from
Brave Ink Press or to purchase books.

The "I can do that!" books™

Time is precious anytime of year—but especially at the holidays. There are so many things you want to do! You can just imagine how it might be—you are serving an elegant dinner on the finest china, gifts are wrapped in flowing ribbons and perfectly-tied bows, your exquisitely decorated cookies are the talk of the neighborhood. However,

The mailman is at the front door,
The children at the back.
The dog is barking wildly (you hope he won't attack!)
You've lost the gift you bought for Mom
When it was on sale.
The ribbon you paid too much for
Is really just too pale.
You pop a cookie in your mouth
Only to remember,
You promised to start dieting
Long before December.

In this book we have given you more than 750 easy-to-make ideas that will help your holiday be happy and stress-free, whether you serve your Christmas dinner on elegant china or on the kids' favorite colorful dishes. Your friends and family will love you and your home as you share laughter and the memories that only Christmas can bring. So no matter how you envision your holiday, it will be wonderful, and you will get everything done to make it a perfect Christmas, just like you always do—

Just in the Nick of Time.

Carol Field Dahlstrom

Contents

How to Use this Book

In this book we have given you more than 750 ideas and projects to make your celebration the best ever. And because we want you to have time to spare, we have made the book easy to use, leaving you plenty of time to enjoy the most wonderful season of the year.

Project Directions

At the end of each chapter you will find step-by-step instructions that have been tested by crafters just like you. And if you are really short of time, look for the 🍁 in front of the title of the project. This little icon means that you can **make this project in less than an hour**, leaving you with even more time for all the things you love to do at holiday time.

Project Patterns

When you are making your project and it calls for a pattern, whenever space allows, we give you a **Full-size Pattern** to complete your project. These patterns are ready to trace or copy as is. If the pattern is bigger than the book page size, we give you the pattern and tell you what percentage to enlarge it. This is easy to do on a scanner or copier.

🍁 Happy Paper

Whether you choose to make P...
Paper Spheres, Christmas Flow...
or Playful Pinwheels, you'll ha...

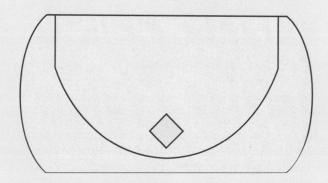

Special Tip Boxes

These tips contain extra information that you might like to know. We give you tips on fabrics, how to store materials, how to involve the rest of the family with the project, and more.

Project Illustrations

When you are creating a project, look for illustrations that we have provided to make the project easier to make. As they say, a picture is worth a 1,000 words! Follow the steps for perfect results.

Special Tip
When making holes in crafting metal using a hammer and small nail or an awl, place a piece of wood or old cutting board under the metal. The hole in the metal will be cleaner and your work table will stay in good shape.

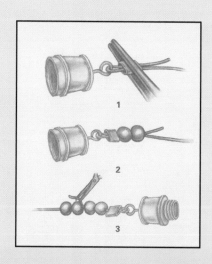

Holiday Recipes

We know that Christmas is a favorite time for baking and cooking. The recipes we share with you have all been tested in kitchens just like yours. The ingredients are easy to find and are family favorites. Because you may want to use the frosting recipes on various cookies and breads, we have put them in boxes so you can find them easily.

Vanilla Powdered Sugar Icing

In a medium bowl, stir together 2¼ cups sifted powdered sugar, 1 tablespoon vanilla, and enough milk (1 to 3 tablespoons) to make spreading consistency. Add the milk gradually until desired consistency is reached. Makes about 1½ cups icing.

And you'll find step-by-step photos to help you make your favorite Christmas cookies.

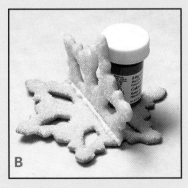

Learning 101

After the how-to and recipes at the end of each chapter, you'll find a quick lesson that pertains to the chapter. For example, learn about different kinds of flatware, candles, and ribbon. Find some quick ideas for cookie and soup toppers, and even some new ideas for hanging ornaments on the tree.

More Ideas

At the end of each chapter you'll also find even more ideas that we share to make your holiday the most memorable it can be. Look for this list of ideas at the end of every chapter.

And at the end of the book you'll find a list of sources to help you locate some of the products you see in this book.

We know you'll enjoy making the projects in the book and we hope all of these special tips and departments help you along the way. Merry Christmas!

Keepsake Ornaments and Trims

Make your holiday tree
the center of attention with
festive ornaments and trims
that you make yourself.
Your family and friends will cherish these
handmade treasures for years to come.

Dress up your holiday tree with handmade ornaments that are sure to become holiday favorites. A simple **Rhinestone Trim** gives a lot of sparkle for the little time it takes to make. Our clever **Star Attraction** shines with a pretty ornament center. Vintage sheet music strikes a perfect chord when you turn it into **Musical Cones** that hang on your Christmas evergreen. A **Peppermint Twist Tree,** made from round candies, glistens on the tree. Make some **Royal Trims** using square stickers and a dusting of glitter. Our little **Snowman Pair** begins as empty glass ornaments—a little paint gives them personality. The **Lovely Pinecone Ornament** is painted and then dipped in glitter for extra sparkle. Instructions for all of the projects start on page 26.

Create **Sparkling Mittens** one at a time or in pairs for everyone on your Christmas list. Made from a simple homemade clay, the shapes are cut from cookie cutters. Choose your favorite shapes and make dozens of these easy-to-make trims.

Tiny rubber stamps, glass paint, and a little fine glitter are all it takes to make **Elegant Stamped Trims**. Use tiny rubber stamps that will roll the paint nicely onto a rounded surface.

Happy Paper Trims fill any Christmas tree with pretty texture and color. Choose from a **Pretty Poinsettia**, a **Paper Sphere**, a **Christmas Flower**, a **Paper Chain**, or a **Playful Pinwheel**. Whichever ones you choose, let the whole family help make these clever trims. Instructions and patterns for all of the projects start on page 29.

So simple to make, yet so pretty on a Christmas tree or displayed on candlesticks, these **Polka Dot Ornaments** can be made in colors to fit your holiday decorating scheme. Just match the glitter to the color of the Christmas ball you choose. Pretty roses, sparkling beads, and metallic-trimmed purchased ornaments combine to make a lovely **Rose and Bead Garland**. The roses are strung while fresh and dried to last all season.

Choose your favorite teacups and tie them with ribbon to hang on a **Pretty Teacup Tree**. Add little groupings of fresh roses and baby's breath. Instructions for all of the projects begin on page 31.

Spell out your holiday wishes using metal words from the scrapbook store. The **Spelled-Out Greetings** are strung together using various lengths of pretty beads.

Tiny yet so striking, our **Magic Metal Trim** forms a tiny picture frame that showcases a favorite holiday stamp. Tiny photos can replace the stamp.

Acorn and Berry Trims are made using real acorns. The **Acorn Ornaments** use just the acorn tops with purchased golden Christmas balls. The **Acorn and Berry Garland** uses acorns and berries that have been drilled. Instructions for all of the projects start on page 32.

A flock of partridges enjoys this holiday pear tree signifying the famous Christmas song. The **Partridge in a Pear Tree Garland** is cut from lightweight natural-colored paper. The wings are cut and glued on the bodies of each bird to make the garland beautifully 3-dimensional. Tiny holes are paper-punched for eyes in each bird.

Tiny Pear Bird Perches are made using small imitation pears with a simple stick perch added. Bits of moss are tucked into the tiny holes. Real orange rind curls complete the pretty tree. Instructions and patterns for the garland and the perches begin on page 34.

Printed papers come in such lovely patterns, textures, and colors. Choose the ones you like to make **Fancy Paper Pocketbooks.** Each little purse has its own personality and is trimmed with varied embellishments. Finish decorating the tree with roses, sheer ribbons, and colorful Christmas ornaments in hues to match. Top the tree with a folded fan topper made from the same pretty papers. Instructions and patterns for the little purses start on page 36.

Create a simple **Nativity Trim** using a clear glass ball, some real straw, and a tiny nativity figurine. Use purchased feathers from the crafts store and a bit of glue to make **Feathered Fancies**. A **Dainty Money Pouch** can be made from any pretty fabric—we chose a gold-motif velveteen. Fill the little pouch with holiday goodies.

Smiling Snowmen perch themselves on a purchased gold ornament. Build your snowmen using air-dry clay. Create **Faux Ribbon Candy** using stripes of oven-bake clay. Trim the edges with sugar-like glitter. Instructions for all of the projects start on page 38.

M Make dozens of these easy **Sparkling Snow Ornaments** using purchased clear glass ornaments and stick-on rhinestones. The loose snow inside the ornament adds winter sparkle. Build your own snowmen using colorful scrapbook papers. The **Printed Paper Snowmen** are cut from paper with colorful brads for details. Create some **Sweet Candy Trims** using colorful gumdrops, candy necklaces, and fine wire. Add some extra sugar on top for glitter. Instructions and patterns for all of the projects start on page 41.

❦ Rhinestone Trims

Catching the light so elegantly, this rhinestone ornament is beautifully simple to make. Start with your favorite colored ornament in any shape and add the sparkle with tiny rhinestones. So easy to make, you'll want to make a set for yourself and a set for special Christmas gifts.

What you need
Solid colored ornaments in a variety of
   shapes (available at discount stores)
Small drinking glass
Toothpick
White crafts glue
Tweezers
Individual rhinestones in various sizes
   and colors (available at theatrical,
   fabric, or craft stores)

What you do
Prop the ornament in the drinking glass to keep it from rolling. Decide on the placement of the rhinestones, referring to the photographs for ideas.

   Using the toothpick, put tiny drops of white glue where you want the rhinestones to be. Depending on how fast you work and how fast the glue dries, try making at least 5 or 6 dots with glue.

   Using the tweezers, pick up a rhinestone and press it into the glue. Continue until all of the rhinestones are positioned on that side of the ornament. Let that side of the ornament dry. Carefully turn over the ornament and add rhinestones to the other side. Allow to dry.

❦ Star Attraction

It's always fun to think of just the right topper for that stately evergreen. Whether you usually have a star at the top of your holiday tree or not, this one is sure to please you. Made from bottle-brush trees, available at discount and craft stores, this topper becomes a much talked about addition to your Christmas tree. Make smaller versions of this clever star for ornaments.

What you need
Five 3½-inch-high bottle-brush trees
Hot-glue gun and hot-glue sticks
1½-inch-diameter foam ball, such as
   Styrofoam
Thirteen ½-inch-diameter round, plastic
   ornaments
Metallic gold chenille stem

What you do
Remove tree bases by turning counterclockwise. Place a small amount of hot glue onto the bottom stem of a bottle-brush tree. Poke the stem into the foam ball and push until the stem is completely into the ball. Continue adding trees in this manner, placing each one next to the last to create a star shape.

   Glue plastic ornaments over the center of the star, covering the foam ball. Build up layers to add dimension, if desired.

   Fold the chenille stem in half, twisting together 2 inches from the ends. Twist ends around the tip of one bottle-brush tree for the hanger.

❦ Musical Cones

Pretty papers turn into magical cones when they change from 2-D to 3-D works of art. Add some ribbon trims and fill them with all the goodies of the season.

What you need
Tracing paper or photocopier
8x8-inch piece of cardstock in desired
   color, or vintage sheet music
Scissors and decorative edge scissors
Paper punch
Crafts glue
Clip clothespin
Gold glitter or ribbon trims
Cording or ribbon for hanging

What you do
Trace or photocopy the cone pattern, *right*. Draw around the pattern onto the chosen cardstock. Cut out. Trim the curved edge with decorative-edge scissors for the gold cone. Form into a cone and glue in place. Use a clothespin to hold edges together until dry. Trim music cone with ribbon trims. Punch a hole in each side of the cone.

   Thread a ribbon or cording through the holes and tie a knot at each end for hanging.

✤ Peppermint Twist Tree

Simple peppermint candies in red and green combine to make the sweetest of ornaments. The candies are placed in a Christmas shape and then baked to melt together forming the pretty trim. Little silver dragees are added in the middle for some extra sparkle.

What you need

Hard, wrapped peppermint candies (red or green)
Hard decorative candies, such as sprinkle decorations or silver dragees
Wire ornament hangers
Waxed paper
Cookie baking sheet

What you do

Preheat oven to 300°F. Lay waxed paper on top of cookie sheet. Unwrap candies and arrange onto waxed paper in desired shape (tree, wreath, candy cane), making sure candies are close together and edges touching. Bake for 3-4 minutes, until candies are softened a bit, watching closely so they don't overbake and flatten. (Oven temperatures vary, so experiment to assess the right length of time for baking.)

Remove from oven and immediately press desired candy decorations into softened peppermint candies. Immediately push wire ornament hanger into the top middle peppermint candy. Allow ornament to cool on waxed paper until hardened. Remove from waxed paper and hang.

Ornaments are fragile, but will keep from year to year if stored carefully.

Note: The candy should never be eaten after making it into an ornament.

Musical Cone Pattern

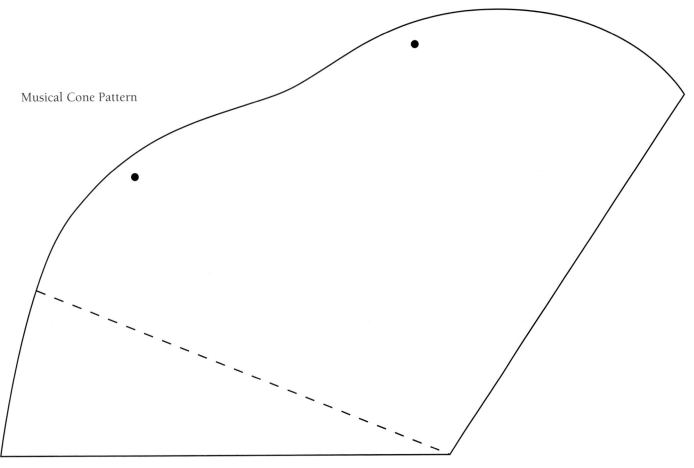

🌿 Royal Trims

Royal Trims are easy and fun to make when you use purchased stickers and a bit of glitter.

What you need

Purchased ornament in desired color
Crafts glue
Fine glitter
Jeweled stickers

What you do

Adhere jeweled stickers on the ball in desired arrangement. Use crafts glue to outline the stickers and dust with glitter.

Snowman Pair

Purchased clear ornaments become playful snowmen in no time with just a little paint and scraps of trims to give them personality-plus.

What you need

Two purchased round glass ornaments with removable tops and flat fronts (available at craft stores)
Rubber band
Transparent glass paints in black, orange, red, and green
Two foam brushes; disposable plate
Small paint brush
Loose white snowflakes (available in bags at crafts stores)
Scrap of ribbon and beaded trim
Crafts glue suitable for glass

What you do

Be sure the ornament is clean and dry. Wrap the rubber band around each ornament about one third down from the top. Following the manufacturer's directions for the use of the paint, use the foam brush to paint the top third of the ornaments starting at the rubber band. Paint one ornament red and one green. Let the paint dry.

Remove the rubber bands. Use the crafts glue to glue the trim around bottom of the painted area. Let dry. Cut a small V-shaped piece of foam from the other paint brush. Place a little orange paint on the disposable plate. Dip the V-shaped piece into the paint and print the nose on each ornament front. Let dry. Use the small paint brush to paint the eyes and mouth. Let dry. Take the top off of the ornament and fill half full with loose snow. Replace top of ornament.

Lovely Pinecone Ornament

Real pinecones decorate evergreens all year long, so this year bring them in to appear on your holiday tree. Add just a little spray paint and some glitter and a single hanger.

What you need

Pinecone
Spray paint in desired pastel color
Glitter to match pinecone
Ornament top from purchased ball ornament
Strong glue, such as E-6000

What you do

In a well-ventilated area, spray paint the pinecone until it is well covered. You may have to spray the pinecone more than one time to completely cover it. Before the last coat dries, sprinkle it with glitter. Allow to dry. Remove the top hanger from a purchased ornament and glue to the top of the ornament. Allow to dry.

Sparkling Mittens

Create mittens that you can hang on the Christmas tree using a simple homemade clay recipe. Use cookie cutters to cut the shapes that you like and add glitter to the cut-out ornaments for extra sparkle. Use a piece of shiny white ribbon to hang the trim on the tree.

What you need

1 cup granulated sugar
3 tablespoons white glue
1 tablespoon glitter
1 teaspoon water
Waxed paper
Paring knife
Rolling pin
Cookie cutters
Round toothpick
Small lengths metallic thread, nylon thread, or narrow cording

What you do

Mix sugar, glue, glitter, and water in small bowl. Lay a square of waxed paper on counter and flatten the ball of crystal dough with hands. Lay another square of waxed paper on top. Gently roll out the dough with a rolling pin to approximately a ¼-inch thickness, keeping the dough between the waxed paper. Remove the waxed paper and cut out desired shapes using cookie cutters. Set aside.

Re-roll remaining dough, as needed. Use a round toothpick that has been cut in half to make a hole at the top of the shape for hanging. Use the edge of a paring knife to smooth out and pat together the edges of the shapes, as needed. Lay shapes out on clean waxed paper to dry overnight. Turn over and dry other side.

Note: This dough is craft dough only and should never eaten.

Special Tip

When packing away fragile, flat, handmade Christmas ornaments at the end of the holiday season, purchase plastic containers that are not too deep. Start with a layer of bubble wrap at the bottom. Lay the ornaments on the bubble wrap and place cut pieces of paper towel rolls beside the ornaments to serve as spacers between layers. This will keep the weight off of the fragile pieces.

Elegant Stamped Trims

Rubber stamps come in all sizes and a variety of patterns, including letters and numbers. Choose tiny stamps, pretty colors of ink, and fine glitter to make these simple and intricate holiday trims.

What you need

Old towel
Purchased matte finish round ornament in desired color
Small rubber stamp in desired design
Old plate
Glass paint in desired color
Glitter to match glass paint color

What you do

Be sure the ornament is clean and dry. Lay it on the old towel. Spread a little of the paint on the plate. Press the rubber stamp into the paint and gently roll it onto the ornament, leaving the design. Repeat as desired on one side of the ornament. Dust with glitter. Let dry. Repeat for other side of ornament.

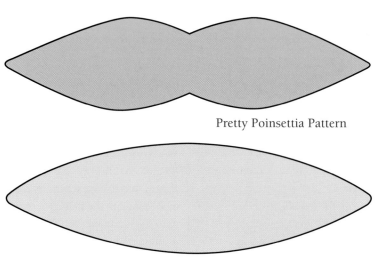

Pretty Poinsettia Pattern

Paper Sphere and Christmas Flower Pattern

Happy Paper Trims

Whether you choose to make Pretty Poinsettias,
Paper Spheres, Christmas Flowers, Paper Chains,
or Playful Pinwheels, you'll have fun creating
these magical shapes.

What you need

Tracing paper or photocopier
Lightweight cardboard
Decorative two-sided papers, such as
*   scrapbooking paper*
Small colored mini brads; ribbon or string
*   for hanging; scissors; small awl*

What you do

For the Pretty Poinsettia, copy or trace
the pattern, ***above right***. Draw around
the pattern on the lightweight cardboard
to make a template. Cut out. For each
flower, trace petal template onto red or
white decorative paper five times. Cut
out shapes. Fold shapes in half, folding
some at slanted, irregular angles. Overlap
pieces, holding them together in the
center. With awl point, make small hole
in center at several places and insert
brads. Tie length of string behind flower
or glue ribbon to back to hang.

For the Paper Sphere, copy or trace the
pattern, ***above right***. Draw around the
pattern on the lightweight cardboard
to make a template. Cut out. For each
ornament, trace sphere template onto

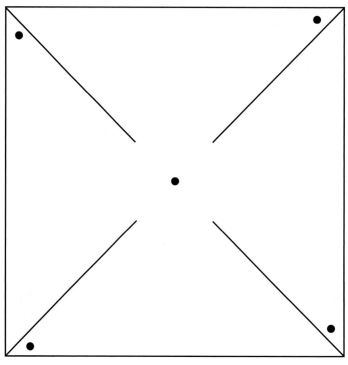

Playful Pinwheel Pattern

double-sided decorative paper five times.
Cut out shapes. Stack pieces and make
a small hole in both ends with the sharp
point of an awl. Insert a colored brad
into holes of one end of all five shapes.
Fan pieces out and insert a second brad
through holes of opposite ends. Work
shapes around to form a sphere. Tie
length of string underneath brad or glue
ribbon to back to hang.

For the Christmas Flower, copy or
trace the pattern, *above*. Draw around
the pattern on the lightweight cardboard
to make a template. Cut out. For each
flower, trace paper sphere template onto
decorative paper five times. Cut out
shapes. Softly fold shapes in half. With
pointed ends of one shape together,
make small hole in ends with awl. Poke
decorative brad through one petal and
overlap with other petals one by one,

poking brad through centers. Fan shapes out. Make 2-4 cuts from fold to center of each petal. Gently bend up alternating cuts to fluff out shape. Attach string or glue ribbon to back to hang.

For the Paper Chain, cut the two-sided paper into strips about ½x3 inches long. Glue the ends together for the first loop. Slip another strip into the loop and glue together. Continue until desired length of chain is finished.

For the Playful Pinwheel, copy or trace the pattern, *opposite*. Draw around the pattern on the lightweight cardboard to make a template. Cut out. Trace around pinwheel template onto two-sided decorative paper. Mark diagonal lines from corners in toward center, stopping about ½-inch from center mark.

Cut out shape and slit along diagonal lines. With awl point, make small holes through paper at points marked on pattern. Bring corners with holes to center hole and insert decorative brad through all holes. Attach string or glue ribbon to back for hanging.

❧ Polka Dot Ornaments

So quick to make yet so elegant to display, these polka dot ornaments are sure to bring "oohs and aahs" from family and friends. Just a little bit of glue and sparkling glitter transform ordinary ornaments into beautiful decorations you'll look forward to year after year.

What you need

White crafts glue
Disposable foam plate
Pencil with new eraser
Plain-colored ornaments
Glitter to match color of ornament
Drinking glass (to hold ornament)

What you do

Pour a little glue onto the disposable plate. Using the eraser end of the pencil, dip eraser into the glue. Dot the glue onto the ornament. See Photo A. Repeat until there are about ten dots. Sprinkle the wet glue with glitter. See Photo B. Put the ornament into the glass to dry. After it is dry repeat for the other side.

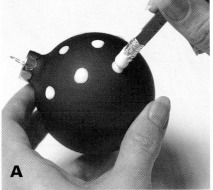

A

B

❧ Rose and Bead Garland

Add an elegant touch to any part of your holiday home with this easy-to-make yet beautiful garland of roses and beads.

What you need

Fresh rose heads
Needle
Dental floss
Small beads
Small purchased ornaments

What you do

Thread the waxed dental floss into the narrow-eyed needle. Start by stringing a bead on the end. Go through the same bead again forming a knot. String the beads (we used small beads interspersed with larger marbled beads), fresh rose heads, and small Christmas ornaments in any order you choose.

Make enough garland for your tree, creating the garland in small sections or make a short section for a mantle trim. Tie a bead at the finished end.

Thread the ribbon through the handle of the cup and tie a knot. Tie the cup onto the tree by first tying a double knot on the tree branch. Then tie a pretty bow. Pull the bow tightly.

For the rose and baby's breath arrangements, cut the rose leaving only about a 3-inch-long stem. Slide the stem into the water vial. Arrange the baby's breath around the rose. Secure it with a rubber band. Using another piece of ribbon, tie a knot and a bow around the rubber band.

Tuck the rose and baby's breath arrangements into the tree branches around the cups where desired.

Pretty Teacup Tree

Gather all of your favorite teacups and display them beautifully by tying them on your Christmas tree. Then add delicate baby's breath and sweetheart roses to complete the beautiful tree.

What you need
Small, preferably lightweight teacups in assorted colors and sizes
1-inch-wide ribbon that ties a tight knot and bow (we used a different color on each cup)
Scissors
Sweetheart roses
Flower vials to hold water (available at floral shops)
Baby's breath
Rubber bands

What you do
For the teacup ornaments, choose ribbon that will not slip when tied. It will take about 1 yard of ribbon to tie a generous bow for each cup.

Spelled-Out Greetings

Spell it out for them as they come to call and they'll feel all the more welcome. Use purchased words from craft stores—you add the pretty beads and ribbon. Try making ornaments in the same way—they send wonderful messages anywhere.

What you need
Purchased word greetings (available at crafts, scrapbook, and art stores)
Small awl or hammer and small nail
24-gauge wire
Beads in colors that you like

What you do
For the door decoration, choose the words that you wish to use. Lay them out to be sure they can be stacked on top of

each other and have a space for making the holes. Use the awl or small nail and hammer to make small holes at the top and bottom at the ends of the words. Measure the wire to fit between the words, leaving enough to loop through the holes and secure. Temporarily loop one end of the wire to keep the beads from falling off. Plan the bead arrangement that you like and thread the beads onto the wire.

Place the end of the wire through one of the holes and twist to secure. Unloop the other wire and place through the other hole. Twist to secure. Hang on doorknob.

To make ornaments, choose the word that you wish. Use the awl or small nail and hammer to make small holes at the top of each end of the word. Measure a piece of wire about 10 inches long. Temporarily loop one end of the wire to keep the beads from falling off. Plan the bead arrangement that you like and thread the beads onto the wire.

Place the end of the wire through one of the holes and twist to secure. Unloop the other wire and place through the other hole. Twist to secure. Hang ornament on the tree.

Special Tip
When making holes in crafting metal using a hammer and small nail or an awl, place a piece of wood or old cutting board under the metal. The hole in the metal will be cleaner and your work table will stay in good shape.

Magic Metal Trim
Easy-to-use crafting metal sheets are layered, decorated with simple designs, and set off with a Christmas postage stamp to make this pretty little ornament.

What you need
3 ¾x4 ½-inch piece light aluminum crafting metal, such as Art Emboss
3 ¼x4-inch piece light copper crafting metal, such as Art Emboss
2 ¼x3-inch piece green scrapbook paper
1 ¾x2 ½-inch piece gold scrapbook paper
Vintage or favorite postage stamp
Piece of craft foam
Double-sided tape
Stylus or ball point pen
½-inch hole punch
Ruler; pencil; scissors
Ribbon for hanging

What you do
Layer the pieces atop each other and mark where they overlap. Decorate or "tool" the metal pieces only where they will show. "Tool" the metal pieces by making designs using the stylus. Lay the metal pieces on top of a piece of craft foam (the craft foam serves as a nice, soft surface for tooling metal), and simply draw designs on the metal. Turn it over when you like the result.

Layer the pieces starting with the aluminum on the bottom, ending with the stamp. Hold them together using double-sided tape. Punch a hole in each side at the top. Hang with ribbon.

Special Tip
When making folded paper garlands, always use strong but lightweight paper and sharp scissors to get a clean and crisp edge. Practice first by folding the paper to see how many thicknesses the scissors can easily cut before starting the final project.

Acorn and Berry Trims

The mighty oak tree provides the inspiration and the shapely acorns for this clever set of trims.

What you need for the Acorn Ornaments

Small purchased gold ornaments
Large acorns
¹⁄₁₆-inch drill bit and drill
Strong crafts glue such as E6000
Ribbon

What you do for the Acorn Ornaments

Be sure the acorns are clean and free of dirt. Remove the cap of the acorn and drill two holes in top of cap about ¼-inch apart. Remove the wire hanger from the gold ball ornament. Put the hanger into the acorn top through the drilled holes and secure underneath. Glue the acorn top to the top of the gold ball. Allow to dry. Hang on the tree with gold ribbon.

What you need for the Acorn and Berry Garland

Large acorns
Tacky crafts glue
Artificial berries
¹⁄₁₆-inch drill bit and drill
Dental floss
Large needle

What you do for the Acorn and Berry Garland

Be sure the acorns are clean and free of dirt. If any of the acorn tops are loose, glue them to the acorn bottoms and allow to dry.

Drill the acorns and the berries through the center using the drill. Thread the floss onto the needle and string the acorns and fruit. Tie at each end.

Partridge in a Pear Tree Garland

Folded lightweight paper is easily cut into a paper partridge garland that makes your holiday tree sing with the season.

What you need

Tracing paper or photocopier
3 ½ x 24-inch strip of lightweight paper in desired color
Pencil
Scissors
Paper punch
Crafts glue

What you do

Trace or copy the patterns, *right*. Set the wing pattern aside.

Fold the strip of lightweight paper accordian-style every 3½ inches. Flatten the paper with your fingers as you fold.

Transfer the pattern to the folded paper being sure that the "fold" edges of the pattern match up with the folds of the accordian-folded paper. Cut out.

Open up the garland and use the paper punch to make a hole for each eye. Fold the edge of the wing and glue in place as indicated on the pattern. Allow to dry.

Tiny Pear Bird Perches

Transform artificial pears into tiny little perches for Christmas birds.

What you need

Small purchased acrylic pears (available at craft stores)
Drill and small drill bit
Sphagnum moss
Toothpick

What you do

Use the drill and bit to make a hole in the front of the pear. Cut or break the toothpick in half. Push into the pear just below the hole. Fill the hole with a tiny pinch of sphagnum moss. Hang on the tree.

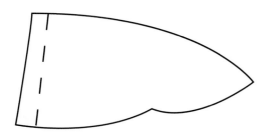

Partridge in a Pear Tree Garland Patterns

Keepsake Ornaments and Trims

Fancy Paper Pocketbooks
*Dress up your tree with a whole collection of
pretty pocketbooks.*

What you need
Tracing paper
Pencil
Printed art or scrapbook papers
Scissors; paper punch
Eyelets and eyelet tools (optional)
Tissue paper
Crafts glue
Clothespin (optional)
Cording or ribbon
*Embellishments such as jewels, fabric
   trims, and buttons*

What you do
Trace patterns, *right and opposite*, and
cut out. Fold printed paper in half and
place the bottom dotted line of pattern
on the fold. Trace onto printed paper
and cut out, cutting only one flap where
indicated. Score and fold on all lines
indicated. For handles, punch holes and
add eyelets if desired or glue cording
under the top flap. Add a small amount
of tissue between layers and glue the
purse edges together. Use a clothespin to
hold the edges while the glue is drying if
necessary. Thread the cording or ribbon
through the punched holes and tie as a
holder. Add embellishments around the
edges and at the clasp, if desired.

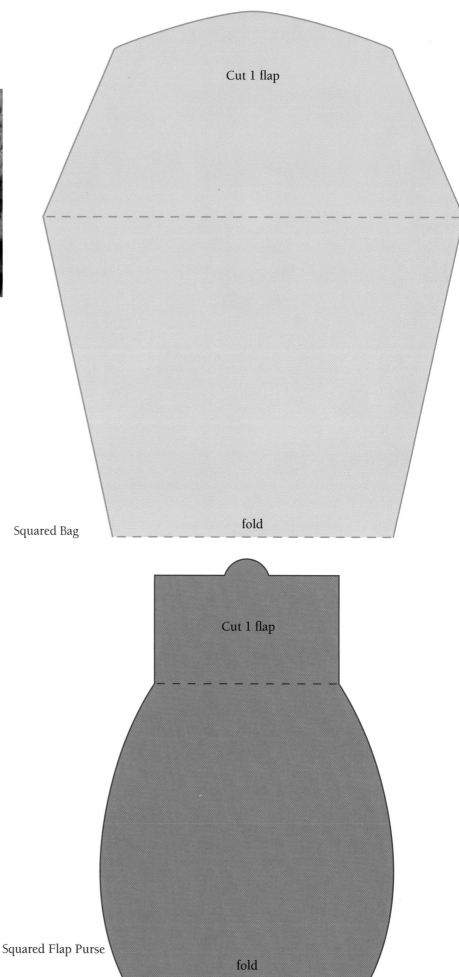

Cut 1 flap

fold

Squared Bag

Cut 1 flap

Squared Flap Purse

fold

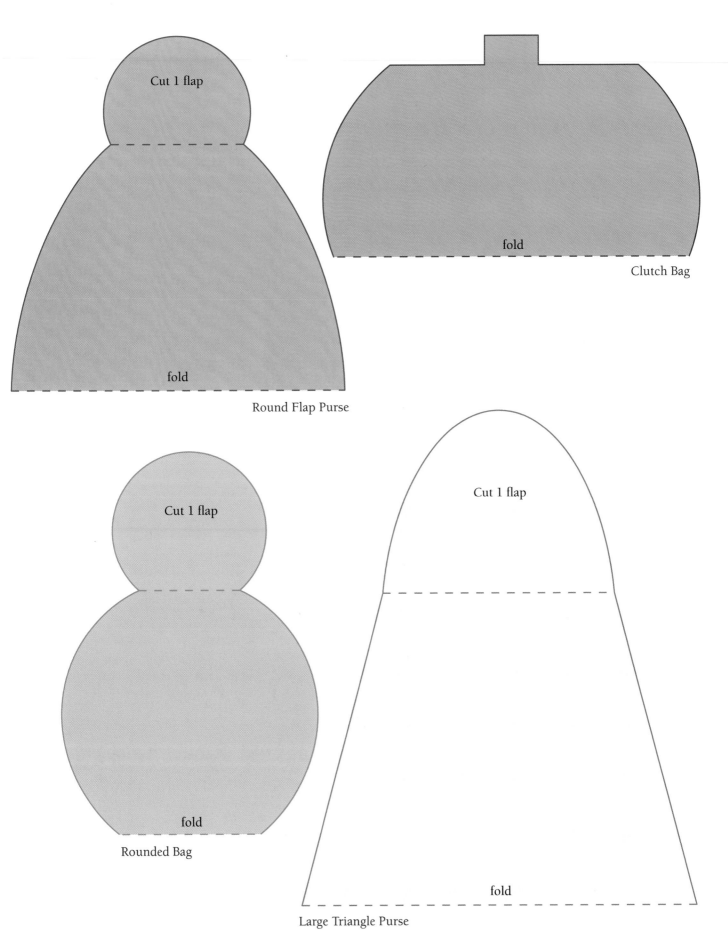

Cut 1 flap

fold

Round Flap Purse

Clutch Bag

fold

Cut 1 flap

fold

Rounded Bag

Cut 1 flap

fold

Large Triangle Purse

🌿 Feathered Fancies

Let nature lend a hand in creating these lovely ornaments. Layer soft, textured feathers on the top of simple gold balls to create a stunning effect.

What you need

Purchased matte finish gold ornaments
Small drinking glass
Tiny feathers (available at crafts stores)
Tacky crafts glue

What you do

Be sure the ornament is clean and dry. Place the gold ornament in the small drinking glass to support it while you work. Arrange one layer of feathers around the top of the ornament and glue in place. Allow to dry. Arrange another layer of feathers on top of the first layer and glue in place. Allow to dry.

Special Tip

When crafting with feathers, place the feathers on a damp piece of terry cloth while working. It will keep the feathers from sticking together or blowing away.

🌿 Nativity Trim

You'll never stop thinking of ideas for filling clear Christmas balls after you begin!

What you need

Purchased clear ornament
Bits of real or artificial straw
Scissors
Small piece of twine
Copper-colored ribbon
Small figurine from a nativity set
Tacky crafts glue

What you do

Be sure the ornament is clean and dry. Take the top off of the ornament and set aside. Cut the hay into little pieces and put inside the ornament. Put the top back onto the ornament. Cut the copper-colored ribbon to desired length and place through ornament top. Tie the twine to the figurine and tie to the ornament top.

Dainty Money Pouch

What a fun surprise to find this sweet ornament filled with special goodies hanging on a frosty evergreen on Christmas morning.

What you need

Tracing paper
Pencil
Scissors
Scrap of velveteen print fabric
Lining to match fabric
Thread to match fabrics
7 inch piece of black cording

What you do

Trace the pattern, *below*, onto tracing paper and cut out. Cut two patterns each from fabric and lining. With right sides together, stitch each set of lining and fabric pieces together at the top edge from markings across top to marking on other side using ⅜-inch seams. Trim, clip at points and across whole top curved edge. Turn right side out and press.

Pin cording handle to top edge of back side of one pouch, having ends extend out seam allowance. With right sides together, stitch the two pouches together at side and lower edges, catching in the handle at top edges. Backstitch at ends of seams to secure handle. Turn right side out and press.

Fill the tiny pouch with desired goodies: wrapped candies, money, tickets to an event, old photos, tiny antiques, jewelry, a single cookie or truffle in a parchment envelope—even a list of things that you love most about that special person.

Dainty Money Pouch Pattern

Faux Ribbon Candy

The bright colors of holiday ribbon candy bring smiles to all who see them. Make this polymer clay version of the popular candy to hang on your tree.

What you need

Polymer clay in desired colors, such as Sculpey
Knife; rolling pin
Waxed paper; toothpick
Crafts glue; white glitter; thread

Smiling Snowmen

Little bits of clay turn into happy winter snowman as they dance upon the ornaments.

What you need

Soft white air-dry clay, such as Crayola Model Magic
Purchased ornaments in desired colors
Acrylic paints in desired colors
Fine line black permanent marker
Iridescent glitter
White crafts glue

What you do

Build the tiny snowmen using the white clay. Stack two small balls of clay (about the size of grapes) atop each other and add two little feet. Add arms. Then add hats, scarves, or other accessories. Fit the snowman onto the ornament as if it is hugging the ball or climbing on it. Let the clay dry on the ornament. This will take about 3 hours. The clay will stick to the ornament until it is dry. Then it will fall away from the ornament.

Paint the snowman accessories with desired paint colors. Add details with markers. While the paint is still wet, sprinkle the snowman with glitter. Let it dry. Glue the snowmen to the ornament. Mix glue and water together in equal parts and paint on the snowman; dust with glitter. Let dry.

What you do

Cut three slices of clay each about ¼-inch thick and about 1x1 inch in diameter. Stack the pieces together. Turn the clay on its side and using a rolling pin, roll out the clay on the waxed paper until it is approximately 1x5 inches long, stretching the clay to reach the length but keeping the layers as even as possible. Use the knife to even off sides and ends so the layered piece is about ¾x4 inches when trimmed. Fold the layered clay back and forth to resemble ribbon candy. Poke a hole in the top with the toothpick. Bake the clay following the manufacturer's instructions. Cool. Coat edges of clay with crafts glue and sprinkle with glitter. Let dry. Put thread in the hole and tie a knot for a hanger.

Note: When stringing gumdrops, use a damp cloth to wipe the needle or wire, preventing it from becoming too sticky.

What you do for the Flower Gumdrop Ornaments

Choose one large gumdrop and seven small ones. Cut six 2-inch-long pieces of wire and one 5-inch-long piece. Push the seven pieces of wire into the large gumdrop like spokes on a wheel. Push the little gumdrops onto the wire; trim extra wire if needed. The long wire goes through the top gumdrop and comes out the other side leaving a long length for a hook.

What you do for the Circle Gumdrop Ornaments

Cut a 9-inch length of wire. String gumdrops onto the wire. Twist ends of the wire together leaving a length of wire for a hook. Lay the ornament on the waxed paper; brush with egg white; sprinkle with coarse sugar. Let dry.

What you do for the Candy Garland

Cut the candy necklace apart. Thread a large needle with dental floss. Tie a piece of candy at one end; string the white gumdrops and candies as desired. Tie a piece of candy to the end to finish.

Note: Never eat candy ornaments.

🌿 Sparkling Snow Ornaments

Pinches of artificial snow inside a clear glass ball adds holiday sparkle.

What you need

*Purchased clear flat-front ornaments
(available at crafts stores)
Loose snow
Small funnel
Snowflake rhinestone stickers
Fine white ribbon*

What you do

Remove the top from the clear ornament. Set aside. Fill the ornament half full with the loose snow using the funnel. Put the ornament top back on the ornament. Place the sticker on the front of the ornament. Put the ribbon through the ornament hanger to hang.

Sweet Candy Trims

Make your tree the sweetest it has ever been!

What you need
for the Flower Gumdrop Ornaments

*Large and small gumdrops
White 24-gauge wire
Old scissors or wire cutters*

for the Circle Gumdrop Ornaments

*Small gumdrops
White 24-gauge wire
Old scissors or wire cutters
Waxed paper
Egg white; coarse sugar*

for the Candy Garland

*Purchased candy necklaces
Small white gumdrops
White dental floss; large needle*

Printed Paper Snowmen

Pretty papers combine to make all kinds of snowman personalities.

What you need

Tracing paper or photocopier
Pencil
4x6-inch piece of printed white scrapbook paper
Scrap of black cardstock
Scrap of printed colored cardstock
Scissors
Crafts glue
Small brads in black, orange, and desired colors
Narrow ribbon

What you do

Copy the snowman pattern, *opposite*, onto tracing paper. Cut out. Trace around the main snowman piece onto the white cardstock paper. Cut out. Trace around the scarf pattern onto the colored paper. Cut out. Make cuts along the end for the scarf fringe.

Choose a hat pattern and trace around on black paper. Cut out. Use crafts glue to adhere the pieces in place. Use black brads for the eyes and mouth. Place an orange brad in backwards for the nose. Use desired color brads for the buttons. Punch a hole in the top and hang on the tree using narrow ribbon.

Special Tip

Try using all different colors of hats, scarves, and buttons on your paper snowmen. To help you decide what colors you like together, draw a simple snowman first and color in the areas with crayons, colored pencils, or markers. Let the children help you decide on colors. Then, together, you can build the perfect snowman.

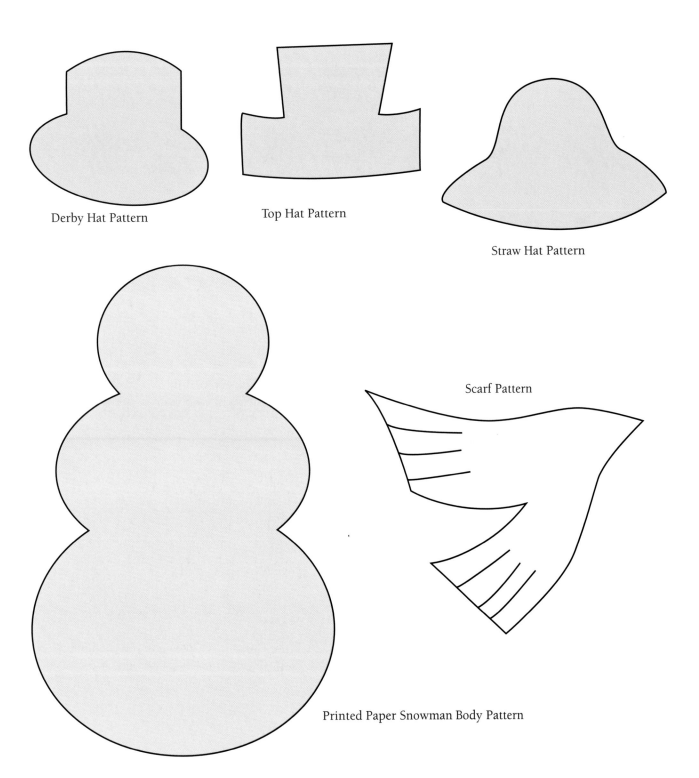

Derby Hat Pattern

Top Hat Pattern

Straw Hat Pattern

Scarf Pattern

Printed Paper Snowman Body Pattern

43

Clever Ornament Hangers 101

Put those hooks aside and try some new ways to hang ornaments on your beautiful holiday tree.

Embroidery Floss
Choose more than one color of floss to string through the hanger—then add a pretty button.

Beads and Wire
String beads of any size on fine wire and curl the end. Then simply bend it for hanging.

Mini-Beaded Garland
A little purchased beaded garland can be cut to the length you want for hanging.

Two Ribbons
Tie narrow satin ribbons together for a quick hanger.

Chenille Stems
Curl these glittery all-purpose chenille stems for a simple and bright hang up.

String of Sequins
Purchased sequins on a string make a quick tie up. Cut to the length you like.

Bow Topper
Before hanging your ornament, tie a pretty bow with a wide ribbon. Then hang up the ornament any way you choose.

More Ideas

Make it a tradition to give a handmade ornament as a gift to a special person each year. Place the ornament in a square box and wrap in plain-colored paper. Write "starting a new tradition" over and over on the outside of the wrapped box using a gold marking pen. Add a pretty bow to the package.

Make copies of favorite photos, cut out, and glue to a star-shaped piece of felt for a simple "from the kids" ornament.

Make small kitchen tools into ornaments by painting them with acrylic paint and hanging them on a small tree in your kitchen.

Fill small florist bags with goodies and hang them on the tree as holiday ornaments.

Use colorful plastic foam sheet shapes (available at crafts stores) and a paper punch to let the children create their own special ornaments. Punch holes around the shapes and string holiday ribbon through the holes, leaving enough ribbon at the end to hang.

Let a child's mitten become a clever ornament. Cut a piece of cardboard just big enough to fit inside the mitten to help keep its shape. Decorate the mitten with fabric paints and colorful jewels. Add a ribbon at the top to hang.

Your pet can be part of your Christmas decorating this year. Choose a favorite picture of your pet and frame it in a small frame. Decorate the edges of the frame with pet stickers. Hang the frame on the tree as an ornament.

The little ones can make a quick kiddie garland by stringing candies and cereals together. Use green waxed dental floss to string candies and cereals with holes, such as fruity cereals, hard circle candies, gummy candies, and oat cereals. Tie the ends in a loop to keep the goodies from falling off.

Spray-paint tiny purchased grapevine wreaths with your favorite holiday color. Glue miniature trims to the wreaths and hang on the tree.

Simple candy canes make great last minute ornaments and fill in large areas on the tree. Simply hook them over the branches between other ornaments.

When choosing a theme for your tree, start with color first. Try to stay within a color family or choose ornaments and Christmas balls that all have the same value. That is, keep bright colors together and pastels together. Patterns and textures work together best if the there is some similarity or repetition in color.

Stunning Centerpieces and Welcoming Tabletops

Make your holiday table reflect
the wonder of the
season with elegant
centerpieces, clever place
settings, and memorable
Christmas favors that you
can create in the blink of an eye.

This holiday make your centerpieces and table settings one-of-a-kind yet surprisingly simple. Create a **Single Bloom Centerpiece** in just a few minutes by snipping off a poinsettia bloom and floating it in water.

Use two hangers in the top of an ornament for a **Festive Place Card Holder**. Add a fabric leaf to a purchased acrylic beaded pear, then make a napkin to match for a **Pretty Place Setting**. A **Goblet Trio** filled with tiny ornaments makes a happy and bright arrangement.

Collect vintage or new Santa light bulbs and make a **Santa Light Display.** Add a little sparkle to a real wishbone and tie it around a napkin for a **Wishful Napkin Ring**. Instructions and patterns for all of these projects start on page 68.

C Choose your favorite color of oversized jingle bells and make them sparkle under a clear glass dome to create **Bells Under Glass**. Add some pretty ribbon around the bottom of the dome stand.

Create centerpieces with a special glow by combining candles and fresh fruit. These elegant, yet oh-so-quick candle arrangements are made by stacking glassware and then surrounding the candle with cranberries or sliced citrus fruits. Whatever shape of candle and fruit you use, your **Fruited Candle Arrangement** will make the season bright. Instructions for all of the projects start on page 70.

Use fresh fruits of the season and a sprinkling of sparkling sugar to create a glorious **Sugared Fruit Tree**. The tree gets its shape by starting with a tree-shaped foam cone.

Simple snowflake motif rubber stamps are dipped into glass paints and lightly pressed onto the glass to make a sweet **Snowflake Vase**.

Adhering purchased beaded ribbon to a simple glass vase makes a pretty **Beribboned Centerpiece**. Just fill the glass with colorful vintage ornaments to complete the look. Instructions for all of the projects start on page 71.

Candles of all shapes and sizes are surrounded with unexpected Christmas pretties. Create any of the **Simply Stunning Candles** in just a matter of minutes. Start with an ivory-colored round candle and surround it with pearls. Use a star-shaped candle and add a sprinkling of jewels. Vintage Christmas lights cluster around a bright red candle. A green pillar candle nestles in golden jingle bells. Simple pink rose petals and frosted evergreen sprigs gather around a trio of pink votives. Instructions for all of the candles start on page 72.

W hite replacement Christmas lights become tiny pieces of art when they are painted with glass paints. Add a name and tie them together for place cards at your holiday table creating **Lights All Around.** Placing a goblet inside a brandy snifter is the secret to the elegant **Pretty Pastel Centerpiece**. Stitch **Holiday 9-Patch Squares** using colorful felted wool. Add decorative stitches to the finished pieces. Instructions for all of the projects start on page 72.

56

T hree rose blooms, orange rind curls, and a touch of glitter is all it takes to make a beautiful **Rose Trio** centerpiece. Choose rose colors that match your holiday decorating scheme. Gather up vintage glassware in Christmas colors of red and gold and arrange on a pedestal or cake plate for a striking **Vintage Centerpiece**. Combine fresh cranberries and bright blooms, hiding one vase inside another, to create a **Holidays in Red Arrangement**. Instructions for the projects start on page 73.

Gather together favorite vintage Christmas light bulbs, or new holiday lights with lots of color and interesting shapes, to create **Christmas Lights Collection**. Simply arrange them in tall glass jars and group them with pieces of evergreen and holly.

Construct the sweetest of little houses and place them side by side for a holiday **Sugar Cube Village**. Then make some little trees to serve as place card holders. Instructions for all of the projects start on page 74.

*D*ress up simple flatware serving pieces with twisted wire and pretty beads. Choose colored wire and beads that accent the theme of your holiday table to create the **Wire-Trimmed Flatware**.

Everyone will love the **Fragrant Candle Ring** you create using cinnamon sticks and coffee beans. The sticks are arranged on a wreath form atop coarsely ground coffee to provide a wonderful aroma. Use a small votive candle with a complimentary fragrance in the center. Instructions for the projects start on page 75.

Create a centerpiece that is sure to become a holiday favorite year after year. This stunning and festive **Fabric Tree Trio** is created using a lightweight fabric and an iron-on stabilizer. The pieces are cleverly designed to slide together and the edges of the branches are tipped with touches of glitter.

Because the trees are 3-dimensional, they combine to look like a winter forest. Place the trees on a square of printed wrapping or scrapbook paper and surround the arrangement with vintage ornaments to complete the look. Instructions and patterns for the project start on page 76.

Make each table setting extra special with napkins that are folded for the occasion. These **Pretty Holiday Napkins** are all folded in different ways with an added table favor. Choose the **Fan Napkin**, the **Royal Napkin**, or the **Rolled Napkin**. Whichever you choose, your holiday table will be dressed up for the big day. Instructions and illustrations for folding the napkins start on page 78.

Single Bloom Centerpiece

Let a single bloom be the showpiece on your holiday table this season. A large dish or punch bowl filled with water is all you need to hold your favorite flower.

What you need

Large bowl such as a punch bowl
Large bloom from poinsettia plant
Water
Glitter

What you do

Wash the bowl or dish and wipe dry. Fill the bowl with water. Cut the poinsettia bloom from the plant, being careful to catch any milky liquid from the plant. Place the poinsettia bloom in the water. Sprinkle with glitter. The bloom will last for 4—5 days.

Festive Place Card Holder

All your guests will love seeing their name displayed on their own take-home ornament, each standing tall in its own beaded holder.

What you need (for two holders)

2 purchased ornaments in desired color (we chose purple)
Rubber cement; gold spray paint
Gold permanent fine-line marker
2 extra hangers from old ornaments
Two 2-inch square beveled mirrors
Six inches of ⅛-inch tiny gold bead garland
Thick white crafts glue; scissors
Purchased place cards

What you do

We made the ornament place cards in sets. One is a reverse color of the other. For the purple with gold star ornament, draw crisscross stars on it using the gold marker. For the purple-starred ornament, use rubber cement to draw crisscross stars on the ornament. Let the rubber cement dry. After it is dry, spray paint the ball gold. Let dry. Using your finger, carefully rub the rubber cement from the ball. The purple from the ornament will show through.

For the place card holder, remove the hanger top from the decorated ornament. Take out the wire loop. Now, take just the wire loop hanger top from an old ornament. Squeeze the bottom two wires together on both loops and put through the same holes into the top of the original one. Put the top back on the decorated ornament. The two loops create a holder for the name card. To make the ornament stand, cut 3 inches of the beaded garland. Form a circle with the beads and glue to the center of the mirror. Let the glue dry. Place the ornament on the circle of beads on the mirror.

Pretty Place Setting

Add your own bit of color and texture to an already beautifully shaped artificial pear by matching the leaf to the cloth napkin that you make yourself.

What you need (for four settings)

Tracing paper
½ yard of printed 45-inch-wide fabric
Pencil
Scissors
Small pieces of fusible interfacing
4 purchased artificial pears
Four 1-inch pieces of 24-gauge wire
Iron

What you do

To make the napkins, cut four 11x11-inch squares from the fabric. Set the fabric scraps aside for the fabric pear leaves.

Turn the edges of the napkin under ¼-inch and press. Turn under ¼-inch again and press. Stitch around the napkins to complete the narrow hem of each napkin.

To make the pear leaf, trace the full-size leaf pattern, *below*. Set aside. Fuse the interfacing between two pieces of the fabric scraps keeping wrong sides together. Trace around the leaf pattern four times onto the fused fabric. Cut out. Carefully open up the flat end of the leaf and insert the wire. Re-iron the fabric together. Remove original leaf from the pear if necessary. Poke the wire that protrudes from the fabric leaf into the pear top. Arrange pear with napkin on the plate. Fold napkin and place on plate beside pear.

Special Tip
When finding fabrics for handmade cloth napkins, be sure and choose fabrics that are made of natural fibers, such as 100% cotton or linen. Natural fibers absorb moisture well and wash and iron nicely. Natural fibers also fold best into crisp folds that hold their shape.

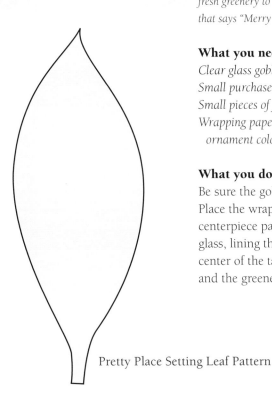

Pretty Place Setting Leaf Pattern

🦌 Goblet Trio
Find your favorite clear-glass goblets and fill them with purchased ornaments and sprigs of fresh greenery to create a colorful centerpiece that says "Merry Christmas!"

What you need
Clear glass goblets
Small purchased ornaments
Small pieces of fresh greenery
Wrapping paper to match or compliment ornament color

What you do
Be sure the goblets are clean and dry. Place the wrapping paper or other centerpiece paper or fabric under the glass, lining the glasses in a row in the center of the table. Add the ornaments and the greenery.

🦌 Santa Light Display
Choose any kind of clear glass dish and display your favorite tiny collections. Miniature Christmas figurines, tiny garlands, little candles, or even wrapped candies are all it takes to make a sweet little arrangement for your table.

What you need
Clear glass dish
Christmas tree lights in Santa shapes
Small pieces of evergreen

What you do
Be sure the dish is clean and dry. Arrange the Santa lights in the dish. Tuck the small pieces of evergreen around the lights. Place on a bright tablecloth or Christmas paper.

❧ Wishful Napkin Ring

A little glitter makes this wishbone sparkle.

What you need

Wishbone
Glue
Paintbrush
Glitter
1-inch-wide sheer ribbon

What you do

Be sure the wishbone is clean and dry. Paint it with glue and dust with glitter. Let dry. Glue glittered wishbone to ribbon and tie onto the napkin.

❧ Bells Under Glass

Collect simple jingle bells and view them under a cake or cheese dome.

What you need

Cake or cheese plate with clear dome top
Jingle bells in desired sizes and colors
Ribbon

What you do

Be sure the dome is clean and dry. Turn the dome upside down and fill with desired sizes and colors of jingle bells. Turn the plate upside down and place over the filled dome. Turn the entire plate and dome right side up. Add ribbon if desired.

❧ Fruited Candle Arrangement

Choose any fresh fruit, pretty dishes, and style of candle for your pretty arrangement.

What you need

Candle in desired color and style
Fresh fruit, such as sliced lemons and limes, cranberries, kumquats, or grapes
Two or more dishes that can be stacked one on top of another

What you do

Wash and prepare fruit. Set aside. Be sure the dishes are clean and dry. Stack the dishes as desired with the smaller one inside the larger one. Place the candle in the smaller dish. Fill the bottom dish with fresh fruit. Add more fruit to the top dish around the candle if desired. Finish arrangement by adding snips of greenery if desired.

Note: Never leave a burning candle unattended.

Sugared Fruit Tree

Frosted with glistening sugar, this decorative fruit centerpiece brings traditional holiday fruits to the table in a new light.

What you need

Plastic foam cone, such as Styrofoam
Clear glass plate
Toothpicks
Small sugared pears; lemon juice
Cranberries
Parsley
Fine and coarse sugar
Egg white; paintbrush

What you do

Place the cone on the plate. Break the toothpicks in half and skewer the fruit. Starting at the bottom of the cone, poke the skewered fruit into the cone. Cut the pears in half if necessary (and dip into lemon juice) to fill the holes. After all of the pears are placed, fill open areas with cranberries and parsley. Brush the entire piece with egg white. Sprinkle with coarse and fine white sugar. Allow to dry. Centerpiece will last approximately 2-3 days.

Note: Do not eat fruit from centerpiece.

🍃 Snowflake Vase

With a simple rubber stamp, a little paint, and fresh flowers you can make a quick holiday centerpiece.

What you need

Plastic plate
Plastic spoon
Clear glass vase with straight sides
Purchased rubber stamp
White or cream-colored glass paints
Fresh flowers and greens

What you do

Be sure the vase is clean and free of finger prints. Pour a small amount of glass paint onto the plastic plate. Smooth it out with a plastic spoon. Dip the stamp into the paint and press onto the glass vase. Repeat stamping the motif until the desired effect is achieved. Let the paint dry. If necessary, bake according to the manufacturer's instructions. Fill the vase with red or white flowers and fresh greens.

Beribboned Centerpiece

Wrapped with ribbon and beads, this lovely centerpiece reflects the sparkle of the vintage ornament collection it holds.

What you need

Glass bowl
Grease pencil
Purchased beaded ribbon trim (available at crafts stores)
Strong crafts glue, such as E6000
Vintage Christmas ornaments

What you do

Position the beaded ribbon on the bowl and mark with grease pencil. Cut the length needed. Make a thin bead of strong crafts glue along the marked line. Glue in place. The glue will dry quickly but the ribbon may slide so watch it carefully for a few minutes. Allow to dry. Fill the bowl with ornaments in coordinating colors.

❧ Simply Stunning Candles

Look around your holiday home to find small trims to make simple candle centerpieces.

What you need

Small items such as jingle bells, jewels, old pearls, vintage Christmas lights, rose petals, etc.
Clear dishes
Candles in desired colors and styles

What you do

Wash and dry the dishes to be used. Set aside. Gather together the items that are to surround the candle. Be sure they are not flammable. Stack the dishes as desired. Place the candle in the top dish. Surround the candle with the pearls, jewels, jingle bells, vintage Christmas lights, rose petals or other objects. Add greenery if desired.

Note: Never leave a burning candle unattended.

❧ Pretty Pastel Centerpiece

To show off those lovely pieces of clear glass that so often get overlooked, try stacking one dish inside another. Here we put a crystal goblet inside a brandy snifter and surrounded the goblet with small ornaments.

What you need

Large brandy snifter
Clear goblet
Small piece of floral tape
Fresh flowers
Small pastel-colored ornaments

What you do

Be sure the clear glass pieces are clean and dry. Adhere the floral tape to the bottom of the goblet. Place the goblet in the brandy snifter. Carefully fill in the space between the goblet and snifter with the small ornaments. Add water to the goblet and add the fresh flowers.

Lights All Around

Your guests will feel more connected when they find their names beautifully written on snow white Christmas tree lights all tied together with a single satin ribbon.

What you need

White replacement Christmas tree lights
Paints suitable for glass painting
Pencil; disposable foam plate
Fine-tipped paintbrush
¼-inch-wide ribbon in two colors

What you do

Wash and dry the bulbs. Try not to touch the glass before painting. Very lightly, write the name of each guest on the light bulbs with a pencil. Have some light bulbs facing one way and some the opposite way. Put the desired colors of paints on the disposable plate. Go over the pencil marks with paint using a fine-tipped paintbrush. Add designs to the bulbs such as evergreen, holly, or ribbons. Allow the paint to dry. Tie all of the bulbs together using a long piece of ribbon, leaving enough room between the bulbs so each bulb can lay in front of each guest's place setting. When the guests leave for home, cut the bulbs apart and give the bulb as a memento of the dinner party.

Holiday 9-Patch Squares

Use wool felt in colors of the season with an unexpected dash of purple trim to make pretty pieced 9-Patch Squares.

What you need

¼ yard red wool felt
¼ yard light green wool felt
¼ yard medium green wool felt
Scissors
Monofilament sewing thread
Purple embroidery floss

How to Felt Wool

Purchase wool felt at a fabric store in the desired color or colors. Wash the entire piece if you are planning to "felt" all of it. If not, cut a piece at least 1½ times larger than the size of the fabric called for. The piece will shrink when washed. Wash the wool felt in hot water and dry on high heat. This will shrink the wool and give it the wrinkled or "felted" texture that you want for the project. Dry in dryer and press lightly.

What you do

Wash each color of wool felt separately in hot water. Dry in hot dryer. Iron flat. For the place mat, cut nine 4x4-inch squares from the pre-washed and dried wool felt. Cut 4 from medium green, 3 from red, and 2 from light green. Lay the pieces in the order desired. Abut the edges and use the zigzag stitch on a sewing machine to sew down the center so that part of the stitch goes on either side of both squares. Add decorative stitches on top of the zigzag if desired, using 3-plies of embroidery floss. Outline the outside edges with the buttonhole stitch.

Make the coasters in the same way using nine 1¼-inch squares.

Note: The pieces may be stitched together by hand rather than using a sewing machine. Simply abut the pieces and sew back and forth across the pieces using a zigzag stitch.

🌿 Vintage Centerpiece

Collect your favorite vintage dishes and display them on a pedestal dish to make a beautiful arrangement in no time.

What you need

Small pieces of vintage glass with red accents
Cake stand on pedestal
Rose petals

What you do

Be sure the glassware is clean. Arrange the pieces on top of the cake stand. Sprinkle the rose petals around the pieces of glassware.

🌿 Rose Trio

Rose blooms and orange rinds are all you need for a sweet little centerpiece.

What you need

Clear glass dish
Water
Rose blooms
Orange rind curls
Fine gold glitter

What you do

Fill the dish with water. Add the rose blooms. Add the orange curls. Sprinkle a little glitter over the arrangement.

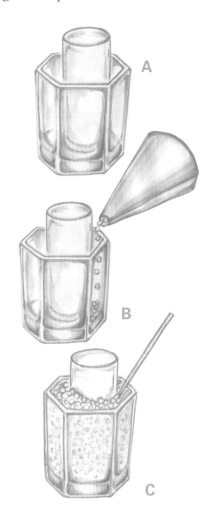

What you need

*Glass jars or other glass containers
    with lids*
*Antique or vintage Christmas lights and
    bulbs, such as bubble lights, lights on
    cording, and Santa light bulbs*

What you do

Organize the lights by color, shape, or
age. Wash and dry the glass jars. Try
different combinations of the lights in
various jars. Arrange with holly and
greens on a glass tray.

❧ Holidays in Red Arrangement

*For an elegant and magical centerpiece, let
cranberries fill a beautiful pitcher showcasing
brightly colored poinsettias and tulips. The trick
is another little container inside the cranberries.*

What you need

Large pitcher or other vase
Smaller container to fit inside pitcher
Floral glue or tacky wax
Fresh cranberries
Cut stems of fresh flowers
Fresh greenery

What you do

Place the smaller container inside
the pitcher. The smaller container
should leave enough room around it
for the cranberries. See Illustration A,
above. Use some floral tacky glue or
wax to secure if necessary. Carefully
place the cranberries between the two
containers using a funnel if desired.
See Illustration B. Use a pick to adjust
the cranberries. See Illustration C. Fill
the inside container with water. Add the
flowers and greenery.

❧ Christmas Lights Collection

*Collect those wonderful lights from years gone
by and display them for all to see.*

Sugar Cube Village

*Tiny sugar cubes stack up nicely to create
miniature houses, tiny trees, and decorated
holiday wreaths. Let the children help create
these magical snow-covered wonders.*

What you need

Sugar cubes
*Heart sugar cubes from sugar cube
    "Bridge Mix"*
Piping Icing (see recipe, opposite)
Waxed paper
Cake decorating bag
*Pink jelly beans, green gumdrops, "cut
    rock" candies, and assorted other candies
    as desired*

What you do

Place Piping Icing in a disposable decorating bag. Snip tip of bag to make a small opening. To make the houses, work on waxed paper and stack the cubes, piping a small amount of icing between each cube. To make a roof section, connect cubes in a rectangle shape. Allow to dry before adding to the house. Add heart sugar cubes on top of house. Attach candy decorations using more icing. To make topiaries, gently reshape green gumdrops into cone shapes. To make the sugar cube trees, arrange a ring of cubes on waxed paper. Add a second ring of cubes on top using icing to connect the cubes. Continue with smaller rings of cubes until there is a single cube for the top of the tree. Use icing to add edible glitter, sprinkles, or colored sugar.

Piping Icing

3 tablespoons meringue powder
6 tablespoons warm water
4 cups sifted powdered sugar
Mix meringue powder and water together until blended. Beat in the powdered sugar until it is frosting consistency.

Special Tip

There are so many things to make using sugar cubes. Try making a wreath by forming a single ring of sugar cubes so the edges touch. Connect with icing. Pipe a squiggle of icing on top of ring. Sprinkle the wet icing with green sprinkles. Use dots of icing to attach a few pink candies for berries. Let dry.

Wire-Trimmed Flatware

Twisted wire and pretty beads combine to make colorful and clever flatware that your guests are sure to admire. Use fine wire in colors that suit your table top colors or use fine wire in silver or gold.

What you need

*Purchased or vintage sugar spoon, pickle fork, and/or butter spreader
24 inches of 24 gauge crafts wire (in desired color)
2 or 3 small beads
Large paper clip
Needle-nosed and square-nosed pliers*

What you do

Fold the 24 inches of wire in half and holding the cut ends with pliers, slip a large paper clip onto the loop end of the wire to begin twisting.

Note: If possible, have another person hold the wire while you twist. When the wire is twisted, remove the paper clip and form a coil with needle nose pliers to begin the embellishment.

Wrap the wire tightly around the handle of the serving piece once, add a bead and wrap around handle again. Continue until two or three beads are added near the end of the handle.

Cut wire to 2 inches and again form a coil with the pliers. Press to lie flat on the handle. If the wraps are not tight enough, use square-nosed pliers to tighten on backside.

Note: Slide off wires before washing utensils. Do not wash in dishwasher.

Fragrant Candle Ring

Cuddle up with a cup of spiced cider and enjoy the delightful fragrance of this easy-to-make candle ring.

What you need

*7-inch plastic foam wreath form, such as Styrofoam
Waxed paper
Tacky crafts glue
Cinnamon sticks
Coffee beans
Coarsely ground coffee
Brown votive candle
Small plate*

What you do

Place the wreath form on the waxed paper. Generously spread the glue on one area of the wreath form and arrange the sticks on the wreath. Glue the coffee beans between the sticks. Continue until the wreath is covered. Spread glue on the sides of the wreath and press on ground coffee. Place wreath on small plate, place candle in center, and surround with coffee beans.

Fabric Tree Trio

Cleverly constructed using printed batik-like green fabric and iron-on interfacing, this little forest of 3-D trees is easy and fun to make. Touches of glitter on the tree edges add a little holiday sparkle. Make a set for yourself or for a holiday gift.

What you need

Tracing paper or photocopier
Pencil
Scissors
⅜ yard lightweight cotton fabric
⅜ yard iron-on stabilizer such as Pellon brand Peltex #72 double-sided fusible ultra firm stabilizer
Glitter

What you do

Trace the patterns, *right and opposite,* using tracing paper or photocopier. Place that pattern on other folded piece of paper to make a full-size pattern for each tree shape. Set aside.

Sandwich stabilizer between wrong sides of fabric pieces. Fuse fabric to stabilizer. Place patterns onto fabric and draw around pattern edges, marking two pieces for each size of tree. Cut out shapes with sharp scissors. Make center slits in each tree shape, cutting the correct length ⅛-inch wide, as follows:

For small tree: Center, measure, mark and cut a 2-inch long slit from the top of one tree. On another tree, make a 4-inch long slit from the bottom up.

For medium tree: Center, measure, mark and cut a 2 ½-inch long slit from the top of one tree. On another tree, make a 4 ½-inch long slit from the bottom up.

For large tree: Center, measure, mark and cut a 3-inch long slit from the top of one tree. On another tree, make a 5-inch long slit from the bottom up.

For all trees, spread a thin line of glue along the outside top edges of the tree. Sprinkle glitter over the glue to decorate and cover up the white edge left when cutting the stabilizer.

Slide the tree with the bottom slit over the tree with the top slit. Embellish with garland, beads, and small ornaments if desired.

Small Tree Pattern

Large Tree Pattern   Medium Tree Pattern

🌿 Pretty Holiday Napkins

Making your holiday table even more special for the holidays is easy when you add cloth napkins that are folded in an elegant style.

What you need

Square cloth napkins in desired color
Iron
Ribbon
Small Christmas item to tuck or tie onto
  folded napkin (optional)

What you do

Start with a clean and flat pressed napkin. Choose the napkin fold that you wish to make and, referring to the diagrams, *right and below,* fold the napkin following the step-by-step illustrations. Use an iron to press between steps if desired.

   If desired, tie or tuck a small Christmas item in or on the napkin or tie on with a ribbon. Lay the folded napkin on the plate.

For the Fan Napkin, fold the napkin in half. Fold the napkin accordian-style starting from the short end. See Illustration 1. Fold the napkin in half again. See Illustration 2. Use a small piece of ribbon to tie a knot about 2-inches from the folded bottom. See Illustration 3. Tie on a small ornament if desired. Fan out the napkin top. See Illustration 4.

For the Royal Napkin, fold the napkin in half and in half again. Lay the napkin with the loose points at the bottom and bring up one layer almost to the top. See Illustration 1. Fold up another layer almost to the first layer. See Illustration 2. Continue folding until all the layers are folded up close to the previous layer. See Illustration 3. Turn the folded napkin over and fold in the sides. See Illustration 4. Tuck a candy cane in the napkin opening if desired.

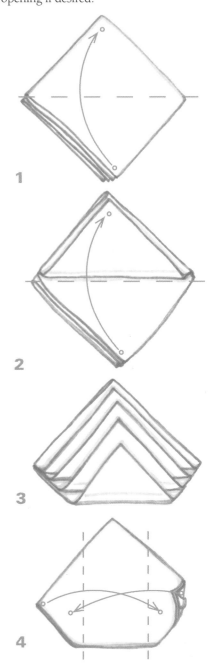

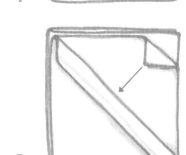

For the Rolled Napkin, fold the napkin in half and in half again. Starting with the upper right corner, roll the top layer down to the middle of the napkin. See Illustration 1. Repeat with the next layer. See Illustration 2. Tuck the rolls under to hold. See Illustration 3. Fold under both sides of the napkin. See Illustration 4. Tuck a Christmas ornament in the fold if desired.

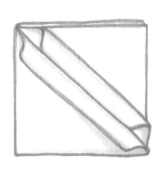

1

2

3

4

Special Tip
To make your table even more festive, make holiday name cards for everyone at the table. Fold a 2x3-inch rectangle of scrapbook paper in half (the long way) and use alphabet stickers as monograms or spell out the entire name on the folded paper. Place the name card above the plate at each place setting.

Flatware 101

Do some research on the types of flatware you have in your "silverware" drawer before you set your holiday table in style.

Silver Plate
Often confused with the more expensive sterling silver, silver plate is made by taking good stainless steel flatware and chemically bonding a very thin layer of silver to it.

Stainless Steel
Stainless steel is an alloy, made with raw materials such as chromium, iron ore, and sometimes nickel. It contains no silver.

Pewter
Pewter was used in flatware pieces centuries ago and is still valued for its rich luster. Pewter dents and scratches easily which is considered part of its patina.

Gold-Plate
As an alternative to silver plated flatware, gold plate can be used over the stainless steel base.

Bone Handle
Flatware items can have bone, pearl, or other composition handles. Usually the main part of these pieces is sterling silver.

Sterling Silver
This flatware contains the most silver. To be marked "sterling silver," federal law requires that it contain at least 92.5% pure silver.

More Ideas

Place vintage ornaments in a large crystal glass bowl and display on the center of the table resting on a favorite doily, holiday napkin, or piece of scrapbook paper.

Showcase favorite round ornaments propped in crystal candlestick holders. Group on a mantel or buffet for a striking effect.

Use an inexpensive rose bowl to float red and white roses with a dusting of glitter for a last-minute holiday centerpiece.

Make a simple centerpiece by filling a glass bowl with star fruit and fresh greens. Add vintage Christmas cards by propping them between the fruits.

Lighting can set the mood for your gathering. Dim the lights or replace bright bulbs with dimmer versions to create soft lighting at your holiday table.

For large parties, fill big copper, tin, or decorative plastic tubs with crushed ice (or snow) and place bottled or canned drinks in the container to keep them cold. Slice oranges, limes, or lemons into the ice or snow for color and aroma. Set the container by the table as part of the room arrangement.

Use holiday fabrics for simple napkins, place mats, table runners, and quick valances. The prints will make your home feel like Christmas in no time.

Use silver everywhere as a decorating statement. Arrange flowers in a silver pitcher, group ornaments in silver bowls, and stand up Christmas cards on a silver tray.

Make a clever centerpiece by putting one small vase inside another larger vase. Put copies of snapshots of Christmases past between the two vases. Fill the inside vase with water and add greens and fresh flowers.

Combine fresh fruits for a stunning centerpiece. Start by setting a pineapple in the center of a large glass plate. Surround it with pomegranates, lemons, limes, and tangerines. Sprinkle fresh cranberries on top of the arrangement. The arrangement will last for about 3 days.

Single pieces of clear glassware make wonderful beginnings for a simple arrangement. Start by stacking the glassware—first a plate or cake plate, then add a small bowl or sauce dish. Place a goblet in the center. Fill the goblet with small ornaments. Try all kinds of combinations using various colors and styles of glassware and china.

Group a variety of candles in a variety of candle holders for a quick mantel or table idea. Keep all of the candles the same color but vary the sizes for an interesting arrangement.

Christmas Cookies and Candies by the Dozens

Sugar, drop, rolled, gingerbread, spice, chocolate, layered, cut-out, frosted, refrigerator, no-bake, and more—you'll find them all in this sweet chapter of cookies and candies.

Make your holiday as sweet as can be with homemade Christmas cookies. **Holiday Icebox Cookies** are sliced and baked in no time. Use pastel sugars and simple stencil designs on the **Pastel Stencil Cookies**. They'll love the combination of pineapple, pecans, and coconut in sweet **White Coconut Fudge**. Have fun decorating some **Retro Reindeer Cut-Outs** in colors that fit the 1950s. The **Gingerbread Cookie Village** has 3-dimensional appeal with a special baked-on stencil recipe. Recipes and instructions start on page 104.

*L*ike little pieces of artwork, **Pretty Paisley Cookies** are decorated with simple dots and swirls. The spice cookie dough is rolled out and cut into paisley shapes before decorating with the pretty frosting.

Sugary Window Cookies are easy to make—just layer colored dough, wrap with plain dough, chill, slice, and bake. The extra sprinkle of coarse sugar on top of the cookie adds a bit of sparkle.

The secret of the beautiful color of **Fruit-Flavored Divinity** is the colored gelatin in the mixture. Make plenty to share with neighbors and friends. Instructions and recipes start on page 107.

Soft and oh-so-sweet **Homemade Marshmallows** are fun and easy to make. Create them in the colors that you like and dust with powdered sugar.

Old-Fashioned Divinity is as white as snow. Decorate it with little pieces of candy, cherries, or favorite nuts for a holiday treat.

Design your **Home-Sweetest-Home Cookies** in the color and style of your own home. Simple squares and triangles make building your home easy. Instructions and recipes start on page 108.

So pretty to look at and so very delicious, **Cran-Apple Crisscross Bars** are made with a rich pie pastry and a lovely cranberry-apple center.

Filled with colorful dried fruits and nuts, **Favorite Fruitcake** can be baked in a small can and cut like a cookie. Serve it with a favorite cup of coffee.

Make an old-fashioned cookie that still brings smiles with its rich buttery flavor and sweet taste. Rolled out and cut into simple shapes, **Country Shortbread Cookies** are decorated using a simple button pressed into the dough before baking. Recipes start on page 110.

Santa comes in all shapes and sizes when you use an assortment of cookie cutter shapes and lots of color and trims. These **Santa Claus Cookies** start with a star cookie cutter, moon cookie cutter, oval cookie cutter, and a diamond shape. The base coat of frosting is painted on and the personality of each Santa comes alive with all kinds of dots and trims.

Recipes for the cookies and frosting, along with decorating tips, start on page 111.

E ven orange peel becomes sweet for the holiday when you make **Candied Citrus Peel.** This sweet confection adds lovely color and texture to your holiday candy tray.

So very fun and pretty, **Polka Dot Cookies** are the perfect gift for any age. The cookies are made from a basic sugar cookie recipe, cut with a simple fluted circle cutter, and frosted with bright colors and polka dots. Recipes and instructions start on page 112.

White and fluffy on the outside, **Coconut Dates** have a sweet surprise of dates, nuts, and cream cheese on the yummy inside.

Everyone will be singing when they see your artwork on the **Twelve Days of Christmas Cookies**. The cookies start with purchased sandwich cookies, then are dipped in vanilla candy coating. You add the clever artwork and variety of color.

Let everyone have fun designing **Pretty Pocketbook Cookies**. The delicious sugar cookies are cut with a purse-shape cookie cutter. Then let your creativity flow with ideas for decorating your dream purse. Make plenty to eat—but save some for a perfect little Christmas gift. Recipes, instructions, and clever decorating tips start on page 113.

Santa will love his milk and cookies when you serve **Christmas Almond Crinkles** on Christmas Eve. So easy to make when time is short, these drop cookies are always a favorite.

The Christmas candy dish will need to be refilled often when you serve crisp and tasty **Cashew Coconut Brittle**. This candy has the delicious added flavor of salty cashews with the sweet coconut.

So very pretty, yet so easy to make, **Pastel Sugar Canes** start with a simple candy cane. The canes are then dipped in candy coating and colorful sprinkles. Recipes start on page 116.

*P*retty as can be, **Cherry Marble Fudge** makes a wonderful gift when presented in a pretty glass dish. The fudge is made using sweet marshmallow creme and stirs together quickly. Crushed cherry-flavored candy canes add flavor and color.

Make colorful **Coconut Gems** in a round pan and cut them in wedges for a holiday treat. So rich and chewy, they will be a holiday favorite.

Everyone will be amazed at your baking talents when you create **Snowflake Stand-Ups**. The snowflake cookie pieces are baked flat and then held together with icing. Recipes and tips for decorating the cookies start on page 117.

Layered candy coatings, both dark and light, are the beginning of easy-to-make holiday **Peppermint Bark**. Choose pretty Christmas candies to decorate all-time favorite **Peanut Butter Beauties**. To make **Poinsettia Pretties**, frost a favorite cut-out cookie and then add a pretty poinsettia using a stencil and fine sugar. A touch of food coloring gives a favorite popcorn ball recipe the Christmas spirit. Add a candy cane in the center of the **Sweet Popcorn Treats** and wrap in cellophane for a perfect little token of the season. So wonderfully unexpected, the flavor of dried cranberries with delicious toffee creates **Cranberry Pecan Toffee**. All of the recipes start on page 119.

Holiday Icebox Cookies

This recipe is a family favorite, enjoyed years ago at holiday time when the "icebox" was a real luxury.

What you need

2 cups fruit (candied pineapple, golden raisins, candied cherries, dates, dried apricots)
2 cups nuts (pecans, walnuts, brazil nuts)
1 cup plus 2 tablespoons butter
⅓ cup granulated sugar
⅓ cup packed brown sugar
1 teaspoon vanilla
1 egg
1⅔ cups flour
¾ teaspoon baking soda
½ teaspoon salt

What you do

Cut up fruits and nuts and place in small bowl. Set aside. In a large bowl, beat butter, granulated sugar, brown sugar, vanilla, and egg. In another bowl, mix flour, soda, and salt. Add fruit and nuts to the flour mixture. Add to the butter and sugar mixture and mix well.

Shape into 2 logs about 2 inches in diameter. Wrap in plastic wrap and foil. Refrigerate dough logs overnight. When ready to bake, remove wraps and cut into slices about ½ inch thick. Place on greased cookies sheet and bake in a 350°F oven for 12 minutes or until lightly brown. Makes about 2 dozen cookies.

Pastel Stencil Cookies

The dark richness of gingerbread combines with delicate pastel sugars to make a delightful Christmas treat.

What you need

Tracing paper
Stencil paper or lightweight cardboard
Crafts knife
5½ cups flour
2 teaspoons ground ginger
2 teaspoons ground cinnamon
½ teaspoon ground cloves
¾ teaspoon baking soda
¼ teaspoon baking powder
1 cup butter, softened
1 cup packed dark brown sugar
1 cup light molasses
2 eggs
Vanilla Powdered Sugar Icing (see recipe at right)
Fine, colored decorating sugars

What you do

Refer to stencil patterns, *opposite*. Trace and transfer to stencil paper or cardboard. Cut around outside shape; cut out colored areas with crafts knife. Set aside.

In a large bowl, stir together flour, ginger, cinnamon, cloves, baking soda, and baking powder. Set aside. In another bowl beat butter with an electric mixer. Beat in brown sugar until fluffy. Beat in molasses and eggs until well combined. Gradually beat

in flour mixture. Use a wooden spoon if dough is too thick for mixer. Divide dough in half. Wrap dough in plastic wrap and chill several hours or until easy to handle. On a lightly floured surface roll out one portion of dough to ¼-inch thickness. Cut out cookies with cookie cutters. Place 1 inch apart on lightly greased cookie sheet. Bake in a 375°F oven for 8 to 10 minutes or until cookies are firm in center. Cool for 2 to 3 minutes on cookie sheet. Remove cookies to a wire rack to cool. Repeat with remaining dough. Makes 4 to 5 dozen cookies.

Decorate about one dozen cookies at a time. With a spatula spread some icing on top of cookies, spreading to, but not over, the cookie edges. Let icing dry 5 to 10 minutes or until surface is just dry to the touch.

Place a cookie stencil carefully on top of just dry icing. Sprinkle some colored sugar over stencil. Carefully lift stencil and shake off excess sugar. Repeat stenciling steps with iced cookies before icing another batch of cookies. Allow sugared cookies to dry several hours before handling.

Vanilla Powdered Sugar Icing

In a medium bowl, stir together 2¼ cups sifted powdered sugar, 1 tablespoon vanilla, and enough milk (1 to 3 tablespoons) to make spreading consistency. Add the milk gradually until desired consistency is reached. Makes about 1½ cups icing.

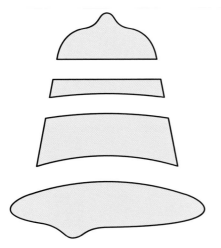

Bell Cookie Stencil

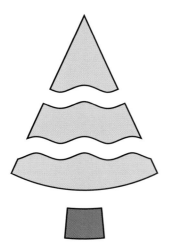

Tree Cookie Stencil

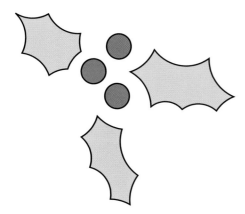

Holly Cookie Stencil

❧ White Coconut Fudge

They'll be coming back for more when they taste these lovely coconut favorites.

What you need

2 cups granulated sugar
⅓ cup white corn syrup
½ cup drained, crushed pineapple
½ cup light cream
1 tablespoon butter
1 teaspoon vanilla
½ cup chopped pecans
½ cup flaked coconut

What you do

In a large saucepan, combine all ingredients except pecans and coconut. Cook, stirring until mixture reaches 235°F on candy thermometer. Cool for 20 minutes. Add vanilla and beat until creamy. Stir in pecans and coconut. Pour into buttered 8x8-inch pan. Cool; cut into squares. Makes 36 pieces.

Special Tip

Make plenty of crushed candy cane pieces in various flavors to have on hand for all kinds of garnishes. Keep the crushed candy canes in canning jars and mark the kind of candy canes used with a tag in a color that matches the flavor. Use the candy to top fudge, divinity, and even hot chocolate.

Retro Reindeer Cut-Outs

Make dozens of these happy reindeer cookies that reflect upon Christmases past. Decorate them in traditional colors or use colors that were popular decades ago.

What you do

Use the Pretty Paisley Cookie recipe, page 107, and cut out with reindeer cookie cutter. (*See Sources, page 239*)

To decorate Reindeer Cookies

Frost baked cookie with a base coat of thinned icing. Then place some thicker, tinted icing in a decorating bag. Snip a very small opening in bag. Add outline and details to reindeer. Add silver or colored dragees and red hots to icing while still wet. Makes 3 dozen cookies.

Note: Silver or colored dragees are for decoration only. Always remove dragees before eating.

Gingerbread Cookie Village

Purchased stencils make these gingerbread houses little works of art.

What you need

5½ cups all-purpose flour
2 teaspoons ground ginger
2 teaspoons ground cinnamon
½ teaspoon ground cloves
¾ teaspoon baking soda
¼ teaspoon baking powder
1 cup butter, softened
1 cup packed dark brown sugar
1 cup light molasses
2 eggs
1 recipe Decorating Dough (right)
1 recipe Meringue Icing (see page 109)
Red and green paste food coloring
House cookie cutters and stencils (See Sources, page 239)
Edible glitter, colored decorating sugar, nonpareils (see Sources, page 239)

What you do

In a large bowl, stir together flour, ginger, cinnamon, cloves, baking soda, and baking powder. In another bowl beat butter with an electric mixer. Beat in brown sugar until fluffy. Beat in molasses and eggs until well combined. Gradually beat in flour mixture. Use a wooden spoon if dough is too thick for mixer. Divide dough in half. Wrap dough in plastic wrap and chill for several hours or until easy to handle. Meanwhile, prepare Decorating Dough. Divide dough into 3 portions. Tint one portion red and another portion green using paste food coloring. On a lightly floured surface roll out one portion of gingerbread dough to ¼-inch thickness. Cut out cookies with large house cookie cutter and use as house shape. Place cutouts 1 inch apart on lightly greased cookie sheet.

To decorate cookies with stencils

Start at top of a cookie and work down. Place a stencil at top of cookie and, with a small metal spatula, spread some Decorating Dough carefully over stencil, being careful not to move stencil (see Photo A). Lift stencil up and wash dough off stencil (see Photo B). Pat dry. Continue with other stencils until cookie is fully decorated. If necessary, trim plastic stencils to allow placing decorations close together. Bake decorated cookies in a 375°F oven for 8 to 10 minutes or until cookies are firm in center. Let cool for 3 minutes on cookie sheet. Remove cookies to a wire rack to cool. Repeat with remaining dough. Makes 1 dozen cookies.

To decorate Gingerbread Houses

Place white or tinted Meringue Icing in a decorating bag with a tip. Pipe decoration onto cookies. Sprinkle wet icing with edible glitter, colored sanding sugar, or small nonpareils. Let icing on cookie dry about 2 hours. To store, arrange flat in single layers with waxed paper between the layers.

To make Decorating Dough

In a bowl beat ¼ cup softened butter with an electric mixer. Add ¼ cup granulated sugar. Beat until combined. Beat in ½ cup light cream or half-and-half. Beat in ⅔ cup flour until smooth.

A

B

Pretty Paisley Cookies

Use your artistic talent to create one-of-a-kind cookies that are sure to please. A spicy sugar cookie dough rolls out easily to make the little shapes. The decoration on the cookies looks sophisticated but is easily achieved using simple dots and lines.

What you need
1 cup butter, softened
⅔ cup dark brown sugar
1 teaspoon baking powder
1 teaspoon ground cinnamon
½ teaspoon ground nutmeg
¼ teaspoon ground cardamom
⅛ teaspoon ground mace
1 egg
1 teaspoon vanilla
2 ⅔ cups all-purpose flour
1 recipe Powdered Sugar Icing (right)
Decorating bags
Paste food coloring in desired colors

What you do
In a large mixing bowl beat together butter, brown sugar, baking powder, cinnamon, nutmeg, cardamom, and mace until light and fluffy. Add egg and vanilla. Beat until well combined.

Gradually add flour and beat until combined. If necessary, cover and chill dough until easy to handle. On a lightly floured surface, roll out dough to ⅛-to ¼-inch thickness. Cut out shapes with desired cookie cutters (*see Sources, page 239*). Place 1 inch apart on lightly greased cookie sheet. Bake in a 375°F oven for 6 to 8 minutes or until edges begin to brown.

Remove to wire rack to cool. When cool, frost with Powdered Sugar Icing, *below*. Makes 3 to 4 dozen cookies.

Powdered Sugar Icing
In a medium mixing bowl place 2 cups sifted powdered sugar. Add 1 tablespoon white corn syrup, 1 teaspoon vanilla, and enough milk to make an easy spreading consistency (1 to 2 tablespoons). Use a thin consistency for painting a base coat on cookies. Use a thicker consistency for piping with a decorating bag. Divide and tint in desired colors. Makes about 1¼ cups icing.

To decorate Paisley Cookies
Mix icing colors using paste food coloring. (We used orange, teal, pink, red, and green.) For brown icing, add unsweetened cocoa powder and some additional milk.

Spread a base coat of thinned red, pink, or white icing onto cookies using a clean artist's paintbrush (see Photo A). Pipe dots, curlicues, and stripes onto cookies using thicker, tinted icing in decorating bags (see Photo B). Let the icing dry.

Sugary Window Cookies

Almost as beautiful as a stained glass window, these cookies are remarkably easy to make. Let the whole family get involved by helping to tint the purchased cookie dough.

What you need
*Purchased sugar cookie dough
  (1 lb. 2 oz. package)
Food coloring
Coarse granulated sugar*

What you do
Divide sugar cookie dough in half. Set one half aside. Divide the other half into 6 portions. Tint each portion with a different food coloring. Roll each tinted portion into a long ½x6-inch

shape. Roll out the uncolored portion of the cookie dough into a rectangle about 4x6-inches and about ¼-inch thick. Stack the colored dough logs inside the center of the rectangle. Wrap the uncolored portion around the colored logs and seal at the seam. Wrap with plastic wrap. Chill for one hour.

Remove the plastic wrap and slice cookies about ½-inch thick. Sprinkle with coarse sugar. Bake according to package instructions. Cool. Makes about 24 cookies.

What you do

In a heavy saucepan, stir together the sugar, corn syrup, hot water, salt, and gelatin. Bring the mixture to a boil. Boil until the mixture reaches a temperature of 250°F on a candy thermometer, stirring occasionally.

Beat the egg whites until stiff. Slowly pour the hot syrup into the egg whites, beating on high until mixture is stiff and loses its gloss. Add vanilla. Add nuts if desired. Drop by rounded teaspoonfuls onto waxed paper. Makes about 35 pieces.

bowl and add vanilla and salt. Set aside. Boil sugar and water to soft ball stage (238°F). Pour syrup slowly over the gelatin, mixing on high speed, until mixture turns very thick and white. Color with food coloring if desired. Pour into a buttered pan. Dust with powdered sugar. Let stand overnight. Cut into small squares. After cutting, dust marshmallows with powdered sugar again if desired.

❧ Old-Fashioned Divinity

As light and smooth as can be, this traditional favorite is always the first to disappear from the holiday candy plate. We've added a touch of peppermint candy to make this recipe just a little sweeter.

❧ Fruit-Flavored Divinity

The secret to these beautiful Christmas-colored candies is just a touch of colored gelatin. Choose the colors that fit your holiday table.

What you need

2 cups granulated sugar
⅓ cup white corn syrup
⅓ cup hot water
3 tablespoons dry raspberry or lime gelatin
¼ teaspoon salt
2 egg whites
½ teaspoon vanilla
½ cup chopped nuts (optional)

Homemade Marshmallows

Who would imagine that this sweet and soft treat is so easy to make? Tint your marshmallows with the colors of the season.

What you need

2 tablespoons unflavored gelatin
¼ cup cold water
1 teaspoon clear vanilla
½ teaspoon salt
2 cups sugar
¼ cup boiling water
Powdered sugar

What you do

Butter an 8x8-inch square glass cake pan. Set aside. Put cold water into a small measuring cup. Sprinkle gelatin into water to dissolve. Pour into mixing

What you need

2 ½ cups sugar
¾ cup white syrup
¼ cup hot water
2 egg whites
Candy cane pieces or nuts (optional)

What you do

In a heavy saucepan, mix together the sugar, white syrup, and hot water; set aside. Beat the egg whites until soft peaks form. Bring the sugar mixture to a boil and boil until thread stage or 248°F on a candy thermometer. Pour the mixture slowly into the egg whites, continuing to beat the egg whites on high speed while adding the syrup mixture. Beat until the mixture forms stiff peaks. Drop by spoonfuls onto a greased cookie sheet. Top as desired. Makes about 3 dozen pieces of candy.

Home-Sweetest-Home Cookies

They'll love the look and know they're home when they see these clever and oh-so-tasty cookies that you made just for them.

What you need

3 cups all-purpose flour
1 teaspoon baking powder
¼ teaspoon salt
1 cup butter, softened
1 cup sugar
1 egg
2 teaspoons vanilla
3 tablespoons milk
1 recipe Meringue Icing (right)
Paste food coloring (pink, leaf green, sky blue, golden yellow) available at discount and craft stores
Disposable decorating bag with coupler and small round and/or star tips, available at discount and crafts stores
Pastel candy decorations and pastel decorating sugars (see Sources, page 239)

What you do

In a large bowl, stir together flour, baking powder and salt. In another bowl beat butter with an electric mixer. Beat in sugar until well combined and fluffy. Beat in egg until well combined. Beat in vanilla and milk. Gradually beat in flour mixture, using a spoon if too thick for mixer.

Divide dough into two portions. Wrap in plastic wrap and chill several hours or until easy to handle. Roll out chilled dough on a lightly floured surface to about ¼ to ⅛ inch thick.

To make house shapes, cut out a few cookies using assorted square cookie cutters or cut squares in 1 to 3 inch square shapes. Cut some of the squares in half, forming triangles to create roof pieces. Arrange the cookies on the baking sheet, overlapping as desired to create different house shapes.

If desired, make a hole for hanging using the end of a straw to poke a hole at the top of the cookie. Bake in a 375°F oven for 8 to 10 minutes or until edges just begin to brown.

Let cookies cool on cookie sheet for 2 minutes. Remove to wire rack to cool.

To decorate Home-Sweetest-Home Cookies

The secret to making these delightful cookies is to layer simple cookie squares and triangles and then to decorate them like your holiday home or the home of your sugar plum dreams. Serve the cookies as they are, or hang them on your Christmas tree to create a cookie village.

When working with many different icing colors over an extended period of time, it is helpful to place the small batches of tinted icing in very small disposable round containers with lids. The icings can be stored overnight in the

refrigerator. Stir icings before using again to restore consistency.

For each color to be tinted, place about ½ cup Meringue Icing in a small bowl. Keep remaining icing covered when not using. Tint icing desired colors with a small amount of food coloring. Gradually stir in a little water, ½ teaspoon at a time, until icing is thin enough to paint on cookies.

Use a clean artist's brush to paint a base coat of desired icing color onto cookie houses. Let dry about an hour. Meanwhile, fit a decorating bag with a coupler and small round or star tip. Fill the bag with some remaining stiff white icing. Pipe house details like windows, doors, holiday decorations, and snow onto cookies. While piped icing is still wet, you may sprinkle with pastel sugars or other candy decorations. Let decorated cookies dry for 1 to 2 hours.

Meringue Icing

In a medium mixing bowl beat together 3 tablespoons meringue powder, ½ teaspoon cream of tartar, 1 teaspoon clear vanilla, and ½ cup warm water with an electric mixer. Beat in 4½ cups sifted powdered sugar on low speed until combined. Beat on high speed for about 5 minutes or until thickened and white. Makes about 3 cups of icing.

Favorite Fruitcake

Here's a fruitcake you'll love to slice and serve with that first morning cup of coffee.

What you need

1 cup butter
1 cup sugar
5 eggs
1 cup grape jelly
½ cup orange juice
2½ cups flour
1 teaspoon baking powder
1 teaspoon cinnamon
½ teaspoon each nutmeg, allspice, cloves, and salt
1 cup candied whole cherries
1 cup blanched unsalted almonds
1 cup pecans
1 cup golden raisins
1 cup raisins
½ cup candied pineapple
¼ cup candied orange peel
¼ cup chopped dates
½ cup coconut
½ cup dried apricots
½ cup additional flour

What you do

In a large bowl, cream together butter, sugar, eggs, and grape jelly. Sift and add the dry ingredients alternately with the orange juice. Mix well. Set aside. In a large bowl mix the dried and candied fruits, nuts, and coconut. Do not cut or

Cran-Apple Crisscross Bars

Made with cranberries and apples and adorned with rich pie pastry, these colorful bars will steal the show. These bars freeze beautifully, so make them ahead of time and present them on Christmas Eve.

What you need

2 cups all-purpose flour
½ cup sugar
½ teaspoon vanilla
2 egg yolks
1 cup butter, softened
2 cups cranberries, frozen
1 Granny Smith apple, finely diced
2 tablespoons orange juice concentrate
1½ cups sugar
2 tablespoons cornstarch
⅛ teaspoon ginger
½ teaspoon salt
½ cup chopped nuts

What you do

For the pastry, in a large bowl, mix the flour, ½ cup sugar, vanilla, and egg yolks. Cut the butter into this mixture. Form into a ball and chill for 1 hour. Grind the frozen cranberries. In a saucepan, mix the cranberries and apples with the orange juice, 1½ cups sugar, cornstarch, ginger, and salt. Simmer on the stove until thick (about 15 minutes). Add the chopped nuts. Chill. Press ⅔ of the pastry into a 9x13-inch pan. Spread with cranberry-apple filling. Roll out the remaining pastry to about a ¼-inch thickness. Cut into narrow (about ½-inch-wide) strips using a pastry wheel. Arrange the strips in a crisscross fashion across the top of the filling. Bake in a 375°F oven for about 20 minutes. Cool and cut into squares or narrow rectangles. Makes about 3 dozen small bars.

chop nuts too finely. Add the additional ½ cup flour to this mixture and stir together. Add to the batter. To prepare the pans, grease with margarine or cooking spray. Line with waxed paper or cooking parchment. Spray or grease the paper again. Pour the batter into pans. Do not smooth the top. Bake in a 300°F oven for about 1 hour or until toothpick comes out clean. Invert onto foil covered rack. Wait 24 hours before slicing. If you want a round cake, grease a clean vegetable can; line the bottom with waxed paper or parchment. Invert pans on rack to cool. Makes 3 standard bread pans or 6 small round cans.

🎄 Country Shortbread Cookies

These deliciously rich cookies have been made for generations using only three ingredients.

What you need
1 cup butter, softened
½ cup plus 2 tablespoons sugar
2½ cups all-purpose flour

What you do
Mix butter and sugar until creamy. Stir in the flour. Make into a ball and chill for 15 minutes. Roll out to ⅓-inch thickness. Cut into 2-inch circles or any other desired shape. To make a design in the dough, press a fancy button into the cookie until a slight impression forms. Bake in a 325°F oven for 12 minutes or until lightly browned. Makes 24 small cookies.

Santa Claus Cookies

Make a Santa star, a Santa moon, or a Santa circle—you'll love them all!

What you need
2 cups all-purpose flour
1 teaspoon baking powder
¾ cup butter, softened
1 cup sugar
1 egg
2 teaspoons vanilla
1 recipe Decorator Frosting (right)
Star, triangle, circle, and Santa moon cookie cutters (see Sources page, 239)
Paste food coloring (pink, leaf green, sky blue, barn red) available at crafts stores
Disposable decorating bag with coupler and small round and/or star tips
Small cinnamon red hot candies or other small candies for nose, eyes, and trims

What you do
In a large bowl stir together flour and baking powder. In another bowl beat butter with an electric mixer. Beat in sugar until well combined and fluffy. Beat in egg until well combined. Beat in vanilla. Gradually beat in flour mixture, using a spoon if too thick for mixer.

Divide dough into two portions. Wrap in plastic wrap and chill several hours or until easy to handle. Roll out chilled dough onto a lightly floured surface to ¼-inch thickness. Cut out with cookie cutter and place on ungreased baking sheet. Bake in a 375 °F oven for 8 minutes or until lightly brown. Cool on wire rack. Makes 24 cookies.

To decorate Santa Claus Cookies
Place about ½ cup Decorator Frosting in a small bowl. Keep remaining icing covered when not using. Tint icing desired colors with a small amount of paste food coloring. Gradually stir in a little water, ½ teaspoon at a time, until icing is thin enough to paint on cookies. Use a clean artist's brush to paint a base coat of icing onto each cookie where Santa's coat or hat will appear. Let dry about an hour. Meanwhile fit a decorating bag with a coupler and small star tip. Fill bag with some remaining white stiff icing. Pipe on fur coat trim, beard, and mustache. Use a small dot of icing to attach candy nose, eyes, and other trims.

Decorator Frosting
In a large bowl beat 1 cup shortening, 2 teaspoons clear vanilla, and ½ teaspoon almond extract. Gradually beat in 2 cups sifted powdered sugar. Beat in 2 tablespoons milk. Gradually beat in 2 cups additional powdered sugar and enough milk (2 to 3 tablespoons) to make a frosting that is creamy and holds a stiff peak. Makes about 3 cups.

Candied Citrus Peel

Full of flavor and fragrance, this treat can be used in cakes and breads or enjoyed as a candy all by itself.

What you need

2 oranges or 2 lemons
6 cups water
2 cups sugar
1 cup water
1 cup additional sugar

What you do

Cut the oranges or lemons in half and squeeze out juice. Boil the rinds in 6 cups of water for 30 minutes. Drain. With a spoon carefully scrape out all the white pith, leaving just the outside peel. Cut the peel into strips with scissors. Mix 2 cups sugar with 1 cup water and bring to a boil. Add cut peel and simmer for 45 minutes, stirring occasionally. Drain using a sieve.

Toss drained peel in 1 cup sugar to coat. Lay out on a single layer of waxed paper to dry overnight. Store in a closed container.

Coconut Dates

So dainty and pretty, these sweet treats add a touch of elegance to any candy dish.

What you need

12 large dates
12 pecan halves
½ cup strawberry cream cheese
1 cup granulated sugar
1 tablespoon white corn syrup
⅓ cup water
2 egg whites
¼ teaspoon cream of tartar
1 teaspoon vanilla
10 small marshmallows
½ cup flaked coconut

What you do

Remove pits from the dates. Fill with strawberry cream cheese. Stuff pecan into the cream cheese. Set aside. In a heavy saucepan, mix the sugar, corn syrup, and water. Boil until the mixture reaches 250°F on a candy thermometer. Set aside. With a mixer, beat the egg whites and cream of tartar on high speed for 1 minute. Slowly pour hot syrup mixture into the beaten egg whites while continuing to beat on high speed. Beat for 5 minutes. Add the vanilla and marshmallows and beat 1 more minute. Dip the stuffed date into the fluffy mixture. Place onto parchment paper. Top with coconut. Serve immediately. Makes 12 candies.

Polka Dot Cookies

Make your Christmas happy and bright with dozens of colorful cookies decorated with simple polka dots.

What you need

1½ cups all-purpose flour
1 teaspoon baking powder
¼ teaspoon salt
¾ cup butter, softened
1 cup granulated sugar
2 eggs
1 teaspoon lemon extract
1 recipe Meringue Icing (see page 109)
Paste food coloring (peach, pink, lavender, orange, lemon yellow, leaf green, blue, neon green, violet, fuchsia pink, golden yellow)

What you do

In a large bowl stir together flour, baking powder and salt. In another bowl beat butter with an electric mixer. Beat in sugar until well combined and fluffy. Beat in eggs until well combined. Add lemon extract. Gradually beat in flour mixture, using a spoon if too thick for mixer. Divide dough into two portions. Wrap in plastic wrap and chill several hours or until easy to handle. Roll out chilled dough on a lightly floured surface to about ¼ to ⅛ inch thick. Cut out shapes with cookie cutters. Use plain or crinkled round cookie cutters to shape cookies.

Place cookies 1 inch apart on lightly greased cookie sheet. Use the end of a straw to make small holes in the top of cookies for hanging. Bake in a 375°F oven for 6 to 8 minutes or until edges just begin to brown. Let cool on cookie sheet for 2 minutes. Remove to a wire rack to cool completely. Makes about 4 dozen 3-inch cookies.

To decorate Polka Dot Cookies

Place about ½ cup Meringue Icing in a small bowl. Keep remaining icing covered when not using. Tint icing desired colors with a small amount of paste food coloring. Use a clean artist's brush to apply a base coat of desired icing colors. Let dry several hours. Use the brush to make small or large polka dots on each cookie. Dry completely.

Pretty Pocketbook Cookies

Pretty purses and bags are fun all times of the year—so decorate this roll-out cookie with designer-style confidence. Add ribbons to the handles to hang them on the tree.

What you need

3 cups all-purpose flour
1 teaspoon baking powder
¼ teaspoon salt
1 cup butter, softened
1 cup granulated sugar
1 egg
2 teaspoons vanilla
3 tablespoons milk
4-inch purse cookie cutter (see Sources, page 239)
1 recipe Meringue Icing (see page 109)
Decorating bags with coupler sets and decorating tips (round, grass tip #233, star)
Paste food coloring (red, pink, lavender) (available at crafts and discount stores)
Decorative sugars
Edible glitter
Small candies; silver dragees

What you do

In a large bowl stir together flour, baking powder, and salt. Set aside. In a mixing bowl beat butter with an electric mixer. Beat in sugar until well combined and fluffy. Beat in egg until well combined. Beat in vanilla and milk. Gradually beat in flour mixture, using a spoon if too thick for mixer. Divide dough into two portions. Wrap in plastic wrap and chill several hours or until easy to handle. Roll out chilled dough on a lightly floured surface to about ¼-inch thickness.

Cut out shapes with 4-inch purse cookie cutter. (*See Sources, page 239*). Use a small sharp knife to cut out a half-circle shape below purse handle.

Place cut-outs 1 inch apart on lightly greased cookie sheet. Bake in a 375°F oven for 6 to 8 minutes or until edges just begin to brown. Let cool on cookie sheet for 2 minutes. Remove to a wire rack to cool completely. Makes 1 to 2 dozen cookies.

To decorate Pocketbook Cookies

Thin about half of the icing to a syrup consistency by stirring in a few drops of water. Divide both thick and thin icings into portions to color. Add paste food coloring to make desired colors. Use the thinned icings to paint a base coat of icing onto the purse cookies using a clean artist's brush.

Add sprinkles and decorative candies, such as silver dragees, to wet icing. Place the thick icings into decorating bags with coupler sets and decorating tips. Pipe decorations and trims onto the cookies.

To make a fringe edge, place icing in a bag with a grass tip to make fringe at edges of a cookie purse.

To make roped handle, pipe icing with a star tip in a rope pattern on the handle of a purse.

To make a swirled print, pull white frosting through solid frosting with a brush or toothpick. Let cookies dry for an hour before serving.

Note: Silver or colored dragees are for decoration only. Always remove dragees before eating.

Twelve Days of Christmas Cookies

You'll welcome the last few days before Christmas with such festive ideas as these candy-dipped cookies. Use the patterns as guides to decorate your twelve-days cookies or make up your own version of each number in the song.

What you need

1 package vanilla cream-filled sandwich cookies (about 4 dozen)
24 oz. vanilla-flavored candy coating
1 tablespoon shortening
Chocolate, green, yellow, and red candy coating discs (about ½ cup each)
4 decorating bags

What you do

In a large microwave-safe bowl place vanilla candy coating and shortening. Microwave on high for 1 minute. Stir. Continue to microwave and stir until melted. With a fork, dip cookies one at a time into melted mixture. Shake off excess candy coating. Place on a wire rack to set up.

Place chocolate, green, yellow, and red candy coating in small microwave-safe bowls or glass custard cups. Melt in microwave for about 1 minute or until smooth when stirred. Place melted coatings in decorator bags. Twist the ends to close the bags. Snip a small opening at tip of each bag.

Pipe designs onto coated cookies, referring to patterns, *opposite*. Or, design patterns to coordinate with song as desired.

Note: If candy coating in bag cools and hardens, place the bag in the microwave and heat for about 30 seconds or until coating is soft.

Twelve Days of Christmas

1 Partridge in a Pear Tree
2 Turtle Doves
3 French Hens
4 Calling Birds
5 Golden Rings
6 Geese a-Laying
7 Swans a-Swimming
8 Maids a-Milking
9 Ladies Dancing
10 Lords a-Leaping
11 Piper's Piping
12 Drummers Drumming

Twelve Days of Christmas Cookie Patterns

🌿 Christmas Almond Crinkles

This simple and delicious drop cookie will be an easy addition to your Christmas cookie tray. Rolled in sugar, these tasty cookies are sure to become year-round favorites.

What you need

⅓ cup butter, softened
⅓ cup almond paste
1 cup sugar
¼ teaspoon baking soda
¼ teaspoon cream of tartar
1 egg
¼ teaspoon almond extract
1½ cups all-purpose flour
Coarse sanding sugar

What you do

In a large mixing bowl beat together butter and almond paste with an electric mixer. Beat in sugar, baking soda, and cream of tartar until well combined and fluffy. Beat in egg and almond extract until combined. Beat in flour. Cover and chill dough until easy to shape. Shape dough into 1-inch balls. Roll in sanding sugar. Place 2 inches apart on lightly greased cookie sheet. Bake in a 375°F oven for 8 to 10 minutes or until tops are cracked and bottoms are lightly browned. Makes 3 dozen cookies.

🌿 Cashew Coconut Brittle

Crunchy, sweet, and with an unexpected heavenly taste combination of cashews and coconut, this candy is hard to resist.

What you need

2 cups sugar
1 cup light corn syrup
½ cup water
½ teaspoon salt
2 tablespoons butter
2 cups cashews
2 teaspoons baking soda
1 teaspoon vanilla
1 cup shredded coconut

What you do

In a heavy 4-quart saucepan, heat sugar, syrup, water, and salt. Bring mixture to a boil; add butter. Using a candy thermometer, stir frequently until mixture reaches 250°F. Add cashews, stirring constantly, until thermometer reaches 305°F. Remove from heat and quickly stir in baking soda and vanilla. Mix well; add coconut. Continue to mix well. Pour into 2 warm, well-buttered baking sheets. Spread thinly. Let cool. Break into bite-size pieces.

🌿 Pastel Sugar Canes

Here's a sweet idea that gets even sweeter. Pure white candy canes get dressed up for the holidays with bright non-pariels.

What you need

12 oz. vanilla candy coating
1 tablespoon shortening
White candy canes
Nonpariels in red, blue, yellow, or
* desired color*

What you do

In a deep microwave-safe bowl place vanilla candy coating and shortening. Microwave on high for 1 minute. Stir. Continue to microwave and stir until melted and smooth.

Holding the straight end of the candy cane, dip the curved edge into the melted vanilla coating. Holding the candy cane over waxed paper, sprinkle with nonpariels.

Prop the candy cane in a tumbler to set up. Continue for the other candy canes. Makes 10 candy canes.

🌿 Cherry Marble Fudge

Red and white swirl happily together to make this pretty Christmas candy a work of art.

What you need

3 cups sugar
1 12-oz. can evaporated milk
1 cup butter
2 7-oz. jars marshmallow creme
2 6-oz. packages white chocolate chips
1 teaspoon almond extract
Red paste food coloring
Cherry-flavor candy canes, crushed
  (about four canes)

What you do

In heavy saucepan, combine sugar, evaporated milk, and butter. Boil for about 12 minutes or to soft ball stage (238°F on a candy thermometer). Remove from heat. Add the marshmallow creme, white chocolate chips, and almond extract stirring until melted. Add food coloring, stirring to swirl. Pour into a greased, foil-lined 9x13-inch pan. Sprinkle with crushed candy canes; chill until set. Remove foil and candy from pan and cut into squares.

Coconut Gems

Rich and chewy, these beautiful little cookies dress up any holiday cookie plate.

What you need

For the base crust
½ cup butter, softened
¼ cup sugar
1¼ cups flour

For the filling

1 cup well-drained, crushed pineapple
1 egg
½ cup sugar
1 tablespoon butter, softened
2 teaspoons cornstarch
1½ cups flaked coconut
¼ cup chopped pecans
Red and green gumdrops (optional)

What you do

In a bowl, mix the base crust ingredients together. Press the crust into greased a 9-inch square pan. Prick with fork. Bake in a 350°F oven for 12 minutes.

Spread the crushed and drained pineapple over crust. Mix remaining ingredients and spread over pineapple.

Bake 20 minutes or until browned. Cool. Cut into squares or triangle wedges. Decorate the tops with red and green gumdrops cut into holly shapes if desired. Makes 16 bars.

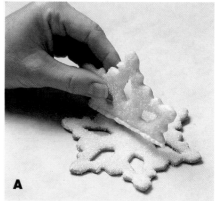

A

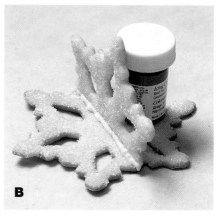

B

Snowflake Stand-Ups

These stunning 3-D snowflake cookies are surprisingly easy to make. A little frosting holds the cookie shapes in place—and of course, no two are alike. Add a dusting of sanding sugar for sparkle.

What you need

4 cups all-purpose flour
1 teaspoon baking powder
1 cup butter
1 cup sugar
⅔ cup light-colored corn syrup
1 teaspoon vanilla
1 egg
1 recipe Meringue Icing (see page 109)
Snowflake cookie cutters (see Sources,
* page 239)*
Decorator bags
Paste food coloring in pastel colors
* (available at crafts and discount stores)*
Sanding sugar in pastel colors

What you do

In a medium mixing bowl combine flour and baking powder; set aside. In a medium saucepan combine butter, sugar, and corn syrup; cook and stir over medium heat until sugar dissolves. Stir in vanilla. Set aside to cool for 5 minutes. Beat in egg. Pour butter mixture into flour mixture. Beat with an electric mixer until well combined. Divide dough in half. Wrap in plastic wrap and chill slightly, about 1 hour, or until dough is firm enough to roll out. On a lightly floured surface, roll one portion of dough to ⅛-inch thickness. For each snowflake cookie, make 2 cutouts of dough. Place 1 inch apart on ungreased cookie sheet. Cut one of the cutouts in half and separate. Repeat with remaining dough. Bake in a 375°F oven for 6 to 8 minutes or until edges just begin to brown. Cool on cookie sheet for 2 minutes. Transfer to wire rack to cool. Makes 2 dozen cookies.

To assemble Snowflake Cookies

Pipe a bead of Meringue Icing onto one cut edge of one of the halved cutouts. Press the cookie half onto a whole cookie that matches (see Photo A). Repeat with each set of whole and halved cookies. Let dry until icing is hard, using food coloring jar as support, for about 2 hours (see Photo B). Stand up the joined cookie pieces and attach the other halved piece of cookie to other side of whole cookie using more Meringue Icing. Repeat with other cookie sets. Let dry 2 hours.

To decorate the assembled Snowflake Cookies

Brush one side of a cookie with some thinned Meringue Icing. Immediately sprinkle with pastel sanding sugar. Repeat brushing and sprinkling until all of the cookie is covered. Set cookie aside to dry.

❦ Peppermint Bark

Everyone loves candy at Christmas time, and this recipe is sure to be a favorite. Layered candy coatings, both dark and light, are the beginning of this simple candy bark. The crushed peppermint candies add pretty color and texture. Make plenty to serve and some extra candy to give as gifts.

What you need

Peppermint candies
12 oz. chocolate-flavor candy coating
1 tablespoon shortening
12 oz. vanilla candy coating
1 tablespoon shortening
Peppermint oil flavoring

What you do

Place peppermint candy canes in a heavy plastic bag. Coarsely crush the candy using a meat mallet or rolling pin. You will need about 1 cup crushed candy. Place crushed candy in a fine wire mesh sifter or strainer and shake to remove fine candy dust. Set aside.

In a large, heavy saucepan melt 12 oz. coarsely chopped chocolate-flavor candy coating and 1 tablespoon shortening over low heat. When melted, remove from heat and pour melted candy onto a foil-lined baking sheet. Gently shake baking sheet to smooth and flatten the candy. Chill for about 30 minutes to set.

Meanwhile, clean and dry saucepan. Melt 12 oz. coarsely chopped vanilla-flavor candy coating and 1 tablespoon shortening in the saucepan over low heat. When melted, remove from heat and stir in ¼ teaspoon peppermint oil flavoring. Pour vanilla candy over the chilled chocolate candy. Spread as necessary to cover the chocolate candy. Immediately sprinkle with crushed peppermint candy. Chill until set, about 30 minutes. Break into pieces to serve or give as gifts. Store in refrigerator.

Special Tip

Wrap individual gifts of Peppermint Bark by sliding a piece of bark into a large parchment envelope or small cellophane bag. Punch a hole in the envelope and thread with ribbon to close. Use a ribbon to close the top of the bag. Add a gift tag to complete the sweet gift.

❦ Peanut Butter Beauties

Favorite peanut butter cookies are dressed up for the holidays with a candy motif.

What you need

1 cup butter
1 cup packed brown sugar
1 cup granulated sugar
2 eggs
1 cup peanut butter
1 teaspoon vanilla
3 cups flour
2 teaspoons baking soda
Pecan halves
Purchased holiday chocolate candies

What you do

In a large bowl, beat together the butter, brown sugar, and granulated sugar. Add eggs, peanut butter, and vanilla. In another bowl, mix together flour and baking soda. Combine with the creamed mixture and mix together until well combined. Dough should be stiff. Roll in balls about the size of a walnut and dip in sugar if desired. Add pecan half or leave plain for candy decoration. Bake in a 350°F oven for 8 minutes. Place chocolate candy in center of plain cookies. Bake 2½ minutes more. Remove from oven and allow to cool on wire rack. Makes 5 dozen cookies.

Place cookies 1 inch apart on lightly greased cookie sheet. Use the end of a straw to make small holes in the top of cookies for hanging. Bake in a 375°F oven for 6 to 8 minutes or until edges just begin to brown. Let cool on cookie sheet for 2 minutes. Remove to a wire rack to cool completely. Makes about 3 dozen 4-inch cookies.

With a spatula, spread some icing on top of cookies, spreading to, but not over, the cookie edges. Let icing dry 5 to 10 minutes or until surface is just dry to the touch. Place a cookie stencil carefully on top of just dry icing. Sprinkle some colored sugar over stencil. Carefully lift stencil and shake off excess sugar. Repeat stenciling steps with iced cookies before icing another batch of cookies. Allow sugared cookies to dry several hours before handling.

Note: Silver or colored dragees are for decoration only. Always remove dragees before eating.

Poinsettia Cookies

So very festive, these stenciled cookies are a snap to make when you use a stencil.

What you need

1¾ cups all-purpose flour
1 teaspoon baking powder
⅛ teaspoon salt
¾ cup butter, softened
1 cup granulated sugar
2 eggs
1 tablespoon water
1 teaspoon almond extract
1 recipe Meringue Icing (see page 109)
Red colored sugar
Silver dragees

What you do

Refer to stencil pattern, *right*. Trace and transfer to stencil paper or cardboard. Cut out colored areas with crafts knife. Set aside.

In a large bowl stir together flour, baking powder, and salt. In another bowl beat butter with an electric mixer. Beat in sugar until well combined and fluffy. Beat in eggs and water until well combined. Add almond extract. Gradually beat in flour mixture, using a spoon if too thick for mixer. Divide dough into two portions. Wrap in plastic wrap and chill several hours or until easy to handle.

Roll out chilled dough on a lightly floured surface to about ¼ to ⅛ inch thick. Cut out shapes with 4-inch cookie cutters. Use plain or crinkled round cookie cutters.

Poinsettia Cookie Pattern

🍂 Sweet Popcorn Treats

Sticky and sweet, popcorn balls are always a favorite. Wrap up extras for sweet gifts.

What you need

1 cup unpopped corn (popped)
2 cups granulated sugar
1½ cups water
½ teaspoon salt
½ cup light corn syrup
1 teaspoon butter
1 teaspoon vinegar
1 teaspoon vanilla
½ teaspoon baking soda
¼ teaspoon cream of tartar

What you do

Remove all unpopped kernels. Place in large cake pan or roasting pan and keep warm in a 225°F oven. Combine the sugar, water, salt, corn syrup, butter, and vinegar. Cook to hard ball stage (250°F on a candy thermometer). Stir in the vanilla, baking soda, and cream of tartar. Mix well. Remove the popcorn from the oven and pour the syrup mixture over the corn. Mix well. Butter hands to easily shape popcorn into balls. Insert a candy cane into center of ball. Cool. Wrap with plastic wrap and tie with a ribbon. Tie a jingle bell at end of the ribbon. Makes about 18 balls.

🍂 Cranberry Pecan Toffee

Sweet brown sugar and just a hint of tangy cranberries make this Cranberry Pecan Toffee one that can't be beat. The texture is crunchy and the look is irresistible. Make plenty to have on hand for the holidays and to give as gifts.

What you need

¾ cup dried cranberries
1 cup butter
1 teaspoon vanilla
1 cup sugar
1 tablespoon corn syrup
3 tablespoons water
¾ cup chopped pecans
½ cup chocolate chips
¼ cup finely chopped pecans for topping

What you do

Butter an 8x8-inch pan and sprinkle the bottom with the dried cranberries. Set aside. Melt 1 cup butter with vanilla in a heavy saucepan; add vanilla.

Blend in sugar, syrup, and water. Cook over medium to high heat until mixture boils and reaches 300°F on candy thermometer.

Quickly stir in chopped pecans. Pour mixture into pan. Sprinkle chocolate chips on top and spread when soft. Sprinkle with finely chopped pecans. When cool, remove from pan and repeat with melted chocolate chips and nuts on the opposite side. Cool thoroughly and break into pieces. Makes about 20 large pieces of bark.

Special Tip

Candies of any kind make great gifts. Choose unique containers to present the candy. Chinese take-out containers, small metal pails lined with foil, even parchment envelopes make easy wraps for sweet treats. Simply add a ribbon and a tag for a much-appreciated gift.

Quick Cookie Toppers 101

Make Christmas cookie decorating a snap when you use these simple ingredients.

Fine Sanding Sugar
Fine sanding sugar comes in all colors and is available at crafts, cooking, and discount stores. Specialty catalogues offer a wide variety of colors.

Metallic Dragees
These very hard little decorative items give sparkle to cookies. Manufacturers suggest removing them before eating the cookies.

Cinnamon Candies
This old-time favorite is great to use as buttons or trims on gingerbread men or Santas.

Coarse Sanding Sugar
This sugar is larger than the more common fine sanding sugar and gives more sparkle and texture.

Colored Coconut
Color plain white coconut with just a few drops of green food coloring for a quick topper.

Chocolate Chips
Simple chocolate chips work well for eyes, buttons, or chocolate polka dots on cookies.

Colorful Nonpariels
These "sprinkles" come in all colors. Put on immediately after frosting the cookie for a colorful decoration.

Gumdrops
Use kitchen shears to cut gumdrops into the shapes you want. Roll between waxed paper to flatten before cutting if you want a thinner shape.

Raisins
Cut raisins in half to use as small eyes, buttons, or other decorations.

Go to the candy shop and choose your favorite chocolate-dipped candies. During the holiday season, there are wonderful shapes and flavors. Add these little treats to your homemade cookie or candy tray for extra sweetness.

Make your Christmas cookies even prettier by adding a drop of red food coloring to the sugar cookie dough. The pastel pink color will add an unexpected holiday touch to your beautifully-decorated cookies.

Give your special homemade Christmas cookies in clever wraps. Try stacking them in a canning jar decorated with stickers, placing them in a small gift bag decorated with rubber stamping, or tying them up in cellophane with a holiday ribbon.

Buy a special plastic tote or box to hold all of your cookie decorating items. Keep colored sugars, couplers and bags, dragees and nonpareils, and other fun items all together in one container to make cookie decorating easier and more fun.

Mix up extra cookie dough and put it in the freezer to have ready to roll out when everyone has a little more time and is ready for some fun in the kitchen. Most sugar cookie doughs can be frozen for up to 3 weeks. Check the recipe for exact times.

Popcorn balls have long been a holiday favorite. Their sticky candy coating compliments the salty, buttery popcorn in a way that no other goodie can. Wrap them individually and pile them in a pretty bowl.

Set the bowl at the front door so guests can take one home after their visit.

If frosting and decorating cookies seems too big a task this year, cut out the shapes with a cookie cutter and brush with milk before baking. Add a sprinkle of colored sugar and the cookies will have a lovely color after baking.

For easy cupcake and cookie toppings, roll gumdrops between pieces of waxed paper. Use tiny aspic cutters to cut holiday shapes and place on top of frosted goodies. The shapes cut easily if the cutters are dipped into warm water before cutting.

For a special Christmas morning breakfast, make pancakes in the shape of bells, Christmas trees, and stars. This simple idea will bring a smile to everyone's face and will set the tone for a wonderful Christmas day.

Purchase small inexpensive Christmas plates in sets of four at your favorite discount store. Separate the set and use the plates to give away an assortment of your best Christmas cookies. You will be giving away two very nice gifts—a pretty Christmas plate and your homemade cookies.

At your holiday cookie exchange, ask each guest to bring the recipe of the cookie they are sharing written out on recipe cards for everyone at the party. Bring a camera and take a picture of the person who made each cookie and then make a scrapbook page with the recipe and the picture of the person that brought it.

Handmade Gifts and Greetings

Bring a smile to everyone on
your Christmas list with gifts you
make yourself. Soft and
sweet baby toys, stylish felted
purses, warm mittens, clever baskets
of goodies, and handmade greeting
cards are just a few of the wonderful
projects in the chapter.

W Whether you favor teddy bears, kitties, or bunnies, you'll love making **Sweet Baby Toys** for the little ones on your Christmas list. Give two gifts in one with a pair of candies surrounded by a simple beaded bracelet creating lovely **Beaded Candles**. A hat and scarf are sure to be a favorite gift. Make a **Simple Hat and Fleece Set** in less than an hour. Everyone loves to get money at Christmas time. Make a clever **Gifty Purse Card** to hold that cash. Present a challenge by giving a **Puzzle-Me Jar**. The knit stitch is all it takes to make **Pretty Spa Cloths**. Instructions and patterns for all of the projects start on page 148.

127

Wrap a plain terra cotta pot with holiday-colored embroidery floss and add a matching tassel for a **Wrapped Up Flower Pot**. Fill the pot with a favorite plant to make a perfect gift.

Give a gift and a card at the same time when you make a **Gifted Greeting**. The pretty parchment paper front spells out the message and holds the vintage handkerchief.

Use your photocopier to help spread holiday cheer. Simply color copy real poinsettia leaves and then cut and glue them together for a **Poinsettia Leaves Card**. The center of the flower is made using tiny golden beads. Instructions for all of the projects start on page 152.

L Line up simple dominoes and glue them to a cork base to create **Polka Dot Coasters**. Finish the clever coasters with a braided trim. Present the coasters in a little gift box to match.

Assemble your own collections of gifts in clever containers to create **Personalized Containers of Goodies**. For the **Fair Player,** use a little pail to hold decks of cards, rules books, poker chips and more. For the **Needlework Lover** gather together embroidery floss, tiny scissors, vintage needles, and other favorite sewing items. Then arrange them in a pretty sewing basket.

For the **Good Cook**, use a sifter to hold favorite kitchen tools. And for the **Handyman**, choose an unused paint can to hold a hammer, paintbrush, screwdriver, and more. Instructions for all of the projects start on page 153.

Sure to bring smiles, embellish packages with some toys on the outside of the box. Perhaps as a clue to what is inside the box, create a **Train Topper** wrap using a minature train with a ribbon track.

Vintage wood toy pieces are glued to the top of a wrapped box for a **Toy Bow**. Stack the wood pieces to resemble a bow and add stickers for a fun embellishment.

Have a little fun with a lovable little duck. The **Just Ducky Trim** is so easy to assemble—the purchased rubber ducky is glued atop a brightly wrapped box and bow. Instructions for all of the projects start on page 154.

Personalize all of your gifts by using purchased gift bags and alphabet stickers to create **Happy Name Bags**. Start with solid-colored bags in the colors that suit your gift. Then use letters to spell out the name of the lucky recipient—have fun using letters of different sizes, colors, and styles to spell out the names. Fill the bags with shred or tissue and put the gifts inside. Add tags that you make yourself, 3-dimensional stickers, or little Christmas ornaments. Instructions start on page 156.

There is no limit to what you can present in a simple canning jar—and after the holidays they can be recycled to use in other clever ways. Create these **Gifts in a Jar** by filling jars with all kinds of goodies. Any knitter would love a jar filled with yarn. Make a cookie jar by decorating the jar with a sticker and filling it with purchased cookies. Mom and baby will love jars filled with tiny socks. Fill a jar for your favorite traveler with toothpaste, stamps, and other traveling companions. A budding artist will appreciate a jar full of paints and some quality brushes. Instructions for all of the projects start on page 156.

*M*aking beaded jewelry is so much fun and so very easy. To make **Pretty Beaded Necklaces**, choose the beads that you like and then simply string them on beading wire using just a few beading secrets. To make a **Simple Alphabet Bracelet** for a little one on your holiday gift list, use elastic filament to string letters of a name with simple pearl accents. Instructions for the projects and tips for beading start on page 158.

Make these easy greetings by the dozen. **Santa Claus Pop-Ups** are made from a simple fold and two little cuts. Add a sticker to complete the card.

Create a **Contemporary Card** using squares of paper all in the same color family. Add a simple sticker to the center of the card.

Don't forget those members of your family with four legs. **Kitty Tuna Treats** will be a favorite for all of your feline friends. Instructions, patterns, and illustrations for all of the projects begin on page 159.

Handmade Gifts and Greetings

F Find some favorite vintage jewelry to add sparkle to your wrapped gifts. Create these lovely **Jeweled Wraps** by simply pinning a brooch or single clip earring to the wrapped package.

Fill them with all kinds of goodies—but first have fun making **Christmas Fun Bags** starting with purchased bags and then adding your own favorite Christmas motif.

Make some clever **Quick Wraps** that are sure to please. Make a silk scarf wrap by bringing the scarf up around the box and tying with a bow. Vintage sheet music makes a wonderful patterned wrap and little dots of paint and glitter spell out holiday wishes on a painted box. Instructions for all of the projects start on page 161.

Give the perfect gift this season with a time-saving **Simple Ribbon-Ready Box**. Anyone would love to have Christmas ribbons ready for wrapping. Add a wider ribbon and simple ornaments to the top of the box.

Use a castaway sweater to make a pretty **Soft Felted Purse** that spills over with style. The sweater is cut apart and "felted" to form the tight wool for the purse. Instructions for the projects begin on page 162.

 Snippets of ribbon and rubber stamped words of the season make a **Pretty Ribbon-Trimmed Card** to be treasured. Stitch up multiple sets of **Fleecy Winter Wear** using your favorite fleece fabric in the colors that you love. Just for fun put the mittens in a jar to present them as a gift.

Carve a simple design in a rubber eraser to make a **Joyous Noel Card**. Let the whole family help you make cards for everyone on your Christmas list. Instructions for the projects start on page 166.

Sweet Baby Toys

You'll be the favorite when you give baby a little stuffed pet to squeeze and love. Made just to fit baby's little hands, the features are embroidered on the fabric giving each one a personality all its own.

What you need

Tracing paper; pencil
Transfer paper in blue and red
¼ yard each of yellow, pink, blue, and green pastel bathrobe velour
Straight pins
Permanent markers in blue and red
DMC cotton embroidery floss: 601, 604, 797, 3839, 3847, 3851
Embroidery needle; scissors; tweezers
Sewing thread to match fabrics; needle
Polyester batting
½ yard each of ¼ -inch-wide pink, green, yellow, and blue pastel ribbon

What you do

Trace pattern of character, *below and opposite,* onto tracing paper. Add another line ¼-inch all the way around to indicate the cutting line. On a single layer of fabric (wrong side up) pin the transfer carbon and trace image of character. Trace around cutting and sewing edges. Remove papers. Fold fabric double with right sides facing. Pin together. Cut out. Remove pins.

With right side facing up on one fabric, place tracing of character to line up exactly with cut edge. Slip transfer paper between fabric and tracing. Trace all embroidery lines. Remove papers. Go over any lines with permanent marker to clarify. Embroider all features (all stitches are worked in 3 strands of floss). Place both sides of fabric together, pin in place (with wrong sides facing). Stitch on stitching line leaving bottom of character open.

Trim fabric, clip at corners, turn inside out. Use tweezers to insert stuffing in ears, arms, and legs. Blindstitch bottom closed. Sew a length of ribbon on neck and form a bow with a separate piece of ribbon. Hand stitch in place. Be sure to stitch down entire ribbon and bow for safety.

CAT
Cross-stitch
✕ 604 Light cranberry (3X)
Backstitch
╱ 601 Dark cranberry (3X)
Satin stitch
╱ 604 Light cranberry (3X)

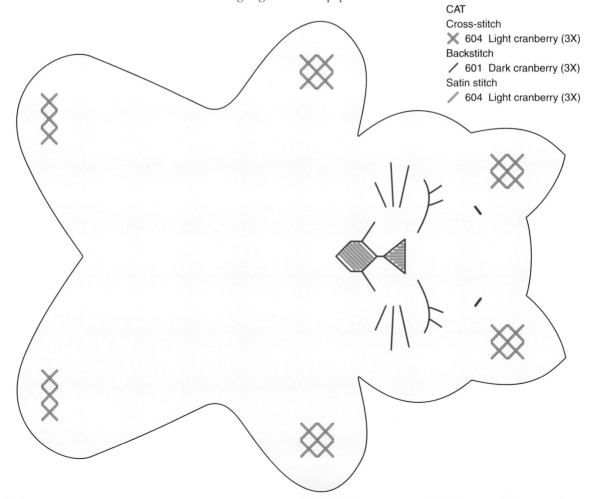

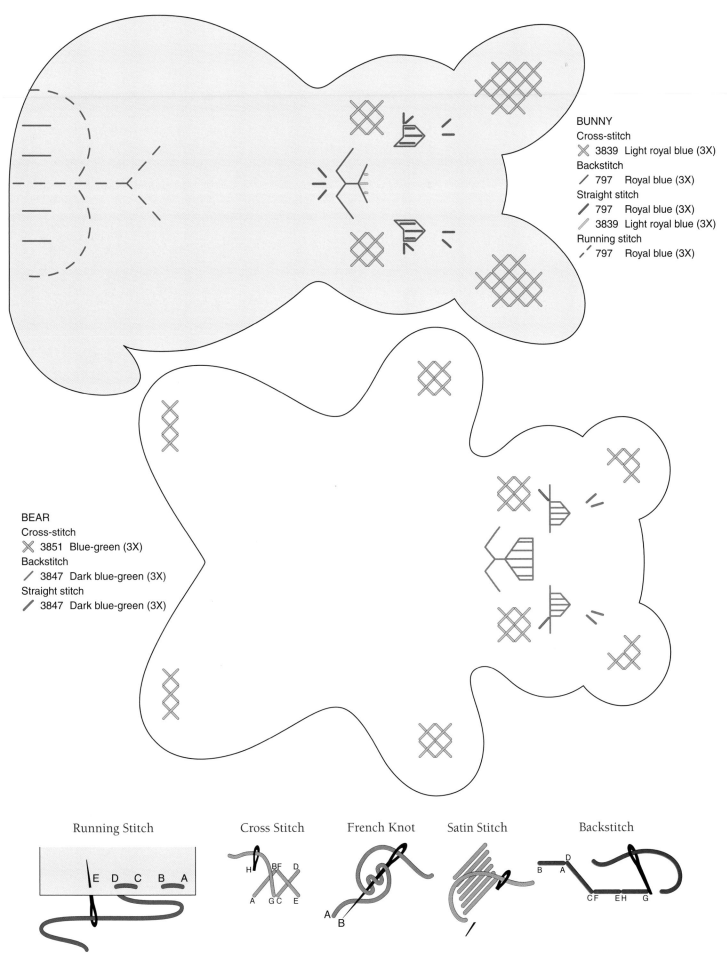

BUNNY
Cross-stitch
✕ 3839 Light royal blue (3X)
Backstitch
╱ 797 Royal blue (3X)
Straight stitch
╱ 797 Royal blue (3X)
╱ 3839 Light royal blue (3X)
Running stitch
╱ 797 Royal blue (3X)

BEAR
Cross-stitch
✕ 3851 Blue-green (3X)
Backstitch
╱ 3847 Dark blue-green (3X)
Straight stitch
╱ 3847 Dark blue-green (3X)

Running Stitch
E D C B A

Cross Stitch
H BF D
A GC E

French Knot
A
B

Satin Stitch

Backstitch
D
B A
CF EH G

🌿 Candle Bracelets

Give these jeweled candle trims (that later become favorite bracelets) by stringing favorite beads onto elastic cording.

What you need

Gossamer elastic beading thread
Scissors
Beads in desired colors and styles
  with holes large enough for thread
Tacky crafts glue
Square candle holders with candles

What you do

Cut the elastic beading thread about 6 inches longer than the finished bracelet to fit around candle. Put a piece of masking tape over the end to keep the beads from falling off.

Begin stringing beads directly onto the elastic in desired order until desired length. Remove the masking tape and tie the two ends together into a double knot, adjusting to fit. Carefully dot a drop of glue on the knot. Allow to dry. Stretch bracelet around candle holder.

🌿 Simple Hat and Fleece Set

So quick to make, you'll want to stitch one for everyone on your Christmas list.

What you need

¾ yard fleece in desired color
Matching thread; scissors
3½x24-inch piece white fleece (for
  snowball hat only)

What you do

Cut off selvages. *For scarf,* cut rectangle with straight or decorative-edge scissors, cutting across the grain of fabric to make a strip 6x60 inches. Fold scarf in half and fringe the ends by making ½ inch cuts through both layers, approximately 3 inches deep. *For hat,* cut piece of fleece 24 inches (crosswise grain, with the most stretch) x 8 inches (lengthwise grain). With right sides together, fold the hat

together to make a piece 12x8 inches. Stitch back seam, using ¼ inch seam allowance, stopping approximately 3 inches from the edge and backstitch. On bottom edge, fold cuff under 3 inches to wrong side of hat. Stitch close to cut edge through both layers of fabric. Turn hat right side out and roll up cuff 2½ inches. Lay hat flat and fringe top edge by making ½ inch cuts approximately 3 inches down. Cut strip of fleece ½ x 12 inches long. Gather top of hat together and hold in your hands while using the fleece strip to tie a tight knot around top fringes. Trim strip even with other ties and fluff fringes.

For snowball hat, cut blue fleece 24 inches (crosswise) x 5 inches (lengthwise). Cut white fleece 24x3½ inches. Connect white fleece to blue fleece by zigzag stitching across the two pieces. Make hat as directed using piece of white fleece to tie top fringes of hat.

🌿 Gifty Purse Card

Everyone likes a little spending money at holiday time. Present it in a tiny little purse card.

What you need

Tracing paper
Pencil; scissors
Purchased card blank (available at crafts
  stores)
5x5-inch piece of cardstock (for purse
  design)
Two clothespins

Crafts glue
Fine gold glitter
6-inch piece of gold cording or ribbon (for
  purse handle)
Gold alphabet stickers
Gold jewel

What you do
Choose a purse pattern from the full-size patterns, *below*. Trace around the entire purse body shape and again just around the flap. There should be 2 pattern pieces when you are done tracing. Cut two purse body shapes and one flap from cardstock.

Glue the sides of the purse body together just along the edges leaving the top open. Use clothespins to hold the purse together while it is drying. Set aside to dry. Glue the flap to the purse front. Set aside to dry.

Use the alphabet stickers to write a Christmas message on the card.

Remove the clothespins from the purse and lay the paper purse on a piece of waxed paper. Use the crafts glue to make a thin line of glue around the flap edge and the sides of the purse. Dust with glitter. Allow to dry. Glue the purse to the purchased card blank front. Tuck and glue the cord or ribbon behind the purse for a handle. Glue the jewel to the front flap. Allow to dry. Fold and tuck the money in the purse.

❧ Puzzle-Me Jar
They'll be surprised and ready for the challenge when they see puzzle pieces nicely collected in a glass jar. Be sure to add a picture of the finished puzzle so they can begin at once.

What you need
*Quart-size canning jar with flat lid and
  screw ring
Small jigsaw puzzle in cardboard box
Plastic bag
Scissors; paper punch
1 yard of sheer 1-inch-wide ribbon
Large bow*

What you do
Take the lid off of the jar. Open the puzzle and place the pieces in the jar. Replace the lid. Set aside. Use the scissors to cut the smaller image from the side of the box. If there is no small image, reduce the size of the image on a scanner or copier. Punch a hole in the corner of the image. Thread the ribbon through the hole and tie onto the jar. Add the bow on top of the jar.

Pretty Spa Cloths
Give a little relaxation to someone you care about with some hand-knit spa cloths. The simple knitted squares are created using only the knit stitch so they take little time to make. Add some favorite spa products with the knitted squares to complete the gift set.

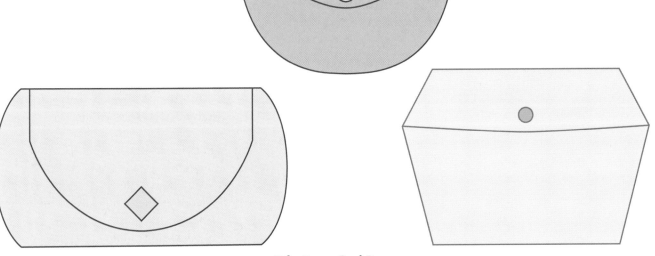

Gifty Purse Card Patterns

Handmade Gifts and Greetings

What you need

SKILL LEVEL: Beginner
FINISHED MEASUREMENTS: Approx
9.5"x11"
Lily Sugar 'n Cream, worsted weight,
100% cotton yarn
1 ball each yellow (00010), Rose pink
(00046) and Teal (01133)
Size 8 (5mm) knitting needles or size
needed to obtain gauge
Gauge: In Garter Stitch (knit every row),
16 sts rows=4'10/cm

Take time to check your gauge

What you do

Cast on 45 sts. Knit every row until
piece measures approximately 9.5" from
beginning. Bind off. Weave in loose
ends on one side of fabric. Make one
cloth in each color.

Wrapped Up Flower Pot

*Wrapped up for Christmas with bright
embroidery floss and embellished with a tassel
trim, this gift of flowers will need no other
wrap. Choose from a variety of beautiful floss
colors to match any decorating scheme.*

What you need

5-inch terra cotta flower pot
White crafts glue
*About 5 skeins of embroidery floss in reds
and greens*
Purchased red tassel
*1 yard of decorator braid (available in the
upholstery section of the fabric store)*
Flower to fit in pot

What you do

Starting at the bottom side of the pot,
apply a thick coating of glue about
2 inches at a time. Begin wrapping the
floss adding glue and changing colors as
desired. Use all 6 strands of floss. At the
top lip, work in the end of a purchased
tassel. Cut the braid in two pieces and
glue to the top rim over the embroidery
floss. Put flower in pot.

🌺 Gifted Greeting

*Make a handmade card to include a gift that
will always be remembered.*

What you need

5 ½x5 ¼-inch piece of green cardstock
5x5-inch piece of red cardstock
Purchased 4-inch vellum envelope
Crafts glue
Gold paint marking pen
Paper punch
10 inches of gold cording
Scissors, pinking shears
Vintage handkerchief
Purchased green envelope

What you do

Glue the red cardstock on the green
cardstock. Cut the top off the vellum
envelope using pinking shears.
Write "A Gift for You!" using the gold
marking pen. Color the top edge of the
vellum using the gold marking pen.
Glue the side and bottom edges of the
vellum envelope on the red cardstock.
Punch a hole at the top two corners
of the card. Knot one end of the cord
and pull through the punched hole to
the other side. Knot the other end of
the cord. Write "Merry Christmas!" at
the bottom of the card with the gold
pen. Fold and tuck the hankie into the
vellum envelope. Trim the edge of the
green envelope with decorative scissors.
Color the flap edge of the envelope with
the gold paint marker.

Poinsettia Leaves Card

*Share a beautiful fresh poinsettia by photo
copying the leaves and reassembling them onto
a holiday greeting to send to a dear friend.*

What you need

Red and pink cardstock
10x5-inch piece of white cardstock
Real poinsettia leaves; scissors
Glue stick; tacky crafts glue
Gold micro beads
Purchased red envelope
Gold paint marking pen

What you do

Carefully snip a few small leaves from your holiday poinsettia. Take them to the copy shop and have them color copied onto red or pink cardstock. Cut out the leaves. Set them aside. Score and fold the white cardstock in half. Use a glue stick to glue the copied leaves onto the front of the folded card. Using the tacky crafts glue, make a large circle in the center of the leaves. Sprinkle with micro beads. Allow to dry. Embellish the flap of the envelope with a gold marking pen.

Polka Dot Coasters

Inexpensive dominoes take on a new role as clever coasters, perfect for that game-playing friend of yours. Arrange the dominoes any way you wish.

What you need

1½-inch wooden dominoes
Small sheet of cork backing
¼-inch-wide metallic red braiding
Scissors
Strong crafts glue, such as E6000

What you do

Cut the cork backing to measure 3¼x3¼ inches. Arrange the dominoes as desired on the cork square. Glue to the cork backing. Finish the edge of the coaster by gluing the braiding around the coaster edge.

To wrap, place the finished coasters in a shallow box. Tie a bow with polka dot ribbon.

For a tag, cut rectangles from black and red paper referring to photo, *above*. Punch holes in red paper to resemble a domino. Glue to black paper; add a name with metallic marker.

Personalized Containers of Goodies

Personalize the gifts you make for everyone on your Christmas list. You can be sure they'll be pleased with the results.

Fair Player

Make good use of old playing cards by decoupaging them to the front of a purchased metal pail. Outline each one with glue and dust with red glitter.

Fill with red tinsel garland, dice, poker chips, cards, and a rule book to keep it all above board.

Needlework Lover

A small sewing basket is the perfect holder for a collection of stitching items. Embroidery floss, needles, and fancy scissors are just a few of the things to put in this gift for a seamstress or cross-stitcher.

from the color copy and glue it around the can. Glue a flat ribbon on both sides of the paper. Fill the can with a hammer, paintbrush, pliers, and other tools. Include a unique hammer cookie cutter to complete the gift.

Train Topper

You'll be right on track with this clever gift topper. See the kids smile when they see part of the gift on the outside of the box.

What you need
Wrapped package
¼-inch-wide ribbon with looped edges
Small train pieces
Crafts glue
Scissors
Paper punch
Paper and stickers for tag

What you do
Glue two rows of ribbon on top of the wrapped package to resemble train tracks. Glue train parts on top of track. Punch a hole in a tag and spell out the name with stickers. Attach to package.

Good Cook
Every good cook will love a sifter filled with great kitchen gadgets. There are so many to choose from in every color to match any kitchen. Fill the sifter with colored spatulas, a variety of whisks, wooden spoons, scissors, a meat thermometer, and more. Tie a curly ribbon around the sifter and add a name tag embellished with silver star stickers.

Handyman
Decorate a quart paint can and fill it with handy tools to have around the house. To make a clever wrap for the container, color-copy screws, nails, and other small toolbox items. Cut a strip

❧ Toy Bow

Find some toss-away pieces from sets of old toys to create a most unexpected and clever bow. It will bring back dear memories and serve as a fun package topper.

What you need

Wrapped package or box
Old toy pieces
Small scraps of ribbon
Alphabet or word stickers
Tacky crafts glue
Scrap of paper and narrow ribbon for tag

What you do

Glue the ribbon pieces to the top of the package, crisscrossing them in the middle. Arrange the toy pieces and glue over the ribbon. Place the word stickers on top of the toy pieces. Add a tag to the package.

Special Tip

Toys and games with lots of pieces often become disorganized. Instead of throwing them away, make a garland from tiny doll shoes, fold play money into tiny ornaments, or tie game pieces onto ribbon bows.

❧ Just Ducky Trim

Create a happy topper for a brightly colored Christmas wrap in no time using a familiar friend that everyone will love.

What you need

Two wrapped packages or boxes
Yellow ribbon
Scissors
Small rubber duck
Tacky crafts glue

What you do

Wrap the boxes as desired or choose purchased boxes in colors that compliment the rubber duck. Colorful pre-wrapped boxes are available at most discount stores.

Stack the packages or boxes and tie or glue them together. Make a bow from the yellow ribbon and glue to the top box. Glue the rubber duck to the top of the bow.

🌿 Happy Name Bags

Wrapping gifts in purchased bags is so easy. This year make it pretty and personal by adding alphabet letters to spell the name of each recipient on the bag. Mix and match letters and colors to spell the name for extra fun.

What you need

Purchased gift bags
*Alphabet stickers in different shapes and
  sizes*
Purchased decorative stickers
Tissue or shred

What you do

Plan the name to be placed on the bag first. Lay the stickers on the bag to be sure the letters fit. Stick the letters to the bag. Add a decorative sticker if desired. Fill the bag with tissue or shred and desired items.

🌿 Gifts in a Jar

Jars aren't just for goodies from the kitchen—fill them with all kinds of gifty surprises! Jars are inexpensive, fun to decorate, and you can recycle them to use again and again!

What you need

*Canning jar in desired size with flat lid and
  screw ring or zinc top (available at grocery
  stores, crafts stores, and discount stores)*
Scrap of paper (to cover lid and make tag)
Scissors
Paper punch
1 yard of ribbon
Item to put in jar

What you do

Remove the inside lid of the jar and trace around it onto the scrap of paper. Cut out. Place the items to be given into the jar. Place the lid and screw top on the jar. Make a tag. Punch a hole in the side of tag and tie on, adding additional tie-ons if desired.

Knitter's Jar

Every knitter loves yarn. So for the knitter on your Christmas list fill a jar with novelty yarn! Tie on some knitting needles to make this jar of knitting a favorite gift.

Cookie Jar

Not all of your Christmas cookies need to be homemade. Purchase your favorites and stack them in a cookie jar for easy giving. Cut a piece of brown paper for the top, trim the jar with 3-D stickers, and tie a ribbon around the top edge. Add a tag to complete the sweet gift.

Baby Stocking Jar

Whether it is a baby boy or baby girl, every little one needs extra stockings! Roll up the tiny stockings and fill the jar with the colors of pink or blue. Cut out a stocking shape from scrapbook paper and make a matching tag. Tie the tag onto the jar with narrow ribbon.

World Traveler Jar

It is always fun to have new cosmetics for that special trip. Fill the jar with much-appreciated travel-size cosmetics. Choose tiny tubes of toothpaste, a small comb, shaving cream—even stamps for mailing a letter back home. Cut a circle from an old map to top it off and add a luggage-gift tag and a little ornament.

Artist's Jar

Fill a jar with all the things that any budding artist will love—brushes, paints, and more. Then add a bold and graphic cut-paper jar topper in bright artist colors. Make a tag and thread cording through the hole to tie the tag onto the jar.

Thread over both wires up to the crimp bead and continue to string the beads until you reach the length you like. See Illustration 2 *below*. End with a crimp bead. Leave at least 4 inches of wire remaining to attach the other end of the clasp. Loop the end of the wire through the other end of the clasp and back through the crimp bead. Squeeze it with the needle-nose pliers as you did at the beginning of your strand.

Feed the wire tail through at least two of the beads and cut off the excess with old scissors or wire snips. See Illustration 3, *below*.

For a quick wrap, present the lovely necklace in purchased white jewelry boxes. Spread with glue and glitter the lid edge. Cut a piece of scrapbook paper just the size of the lid, glue it to the top, and decorate as you wish to make a pretty gift box for your jewelry.

Pretty Beaded Necklaces

Choose beads in the styles and colors that you like and make a stunning necklace.

What you need

Beading wire, such as .018" 16# 12kg
Old scissors or wire snips
Needle-nosed pliers
Necklace clasps; crimp beads
Assortment of beads that you like
Small square of felt to arrange the beads

What you do

Cut the wire the length you want your strand to be, plus 6 inches. Common necklace lengths are 14, 16, and 18 inches. Set aside. Lay out the piece of felt and arrange the beads on the felt in the order that you plan to string them. The felt will keep the beads from rolling around. Choose the type of clasp that you want to use. There are many kinds and all work well. Separate the clasp and place one piece at each end of the beads that you have on the felt. Place a crimp bead at each end of the row of beads beside the clasp piece.

Thread one end of the wire through a crimp bead, then through one end of the clasp and then back through the crimp bead leaving about ½ inch of the wire tail. Using the needle-nosed pliers, squeeze the crimp head to keep the wire from slipping out. See Illustration 1, *right*. Start stringing the beads you have laid out on the piece of felt in the order that you decided.

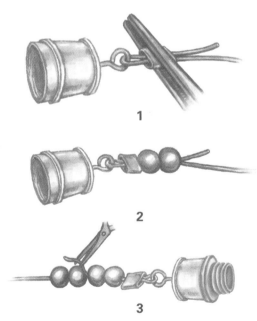

1

2

3

Simple Alphabet Bracelet

Everyone loves to wear beads—and especially when it spells out a name! Make one for everyone on your Chrismtas list.

What you need

Gossamer elastic beading thread
Scissors
Alphabet beads in desired colors and styles with holes large enough for thread
Small pearlized beads in desired color with holes large enough for thread
Tacky crafts glue

What you do

Cut the elastic beading thread to about 6 inches longer than the finished bracelet. Put a piece of masking tape over the end to keep the beads from falling off.

Beginning stringing pearl beads and alphabet beads directly onto the elastic thread in desired order, spelling the desired name. Remove the masking tape and tie the two ends together into a double knot adjusting to fit if necessary. Carefully dot a drop of glue on the knot. Allow to dry.

Santa Claus Pop-Ups

Make Santa the star attraction when you have him take center stage in these easy-to-make pop-out cards. Use double-sided tape to add some glittery bricks for the chimney.

What you need

7x7-inch piece of red or gold vellum or lightweight paper
Scissors; pencil
Double-stick tape
Fine glitter in desired color
Large Santa sticker

What you do

Fold the paper in quarters, referring to Illustration 1, *below*. Open up one fold and with the fold at the left, mark an A and B in the top and bottom corners, see Illustration 2, *below*. Referring to measurements in Diagram A, *right*, make two cuts on the folded edge. Open up the card, see Illustration 3, *below*. Fold the top (A) to the back. Pop out the cut section, see Illustration 4, *below*. Turn the card vertically so the pop-up section comes out the front. Cut the double-stick tape into small rectangles and place on the top of the card to resemble bricks. Peel off the tape front and dust with glitter. Add the large Santa sticker to the front of the pop-up card.

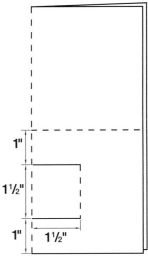

1"

1½"

1"   1½"

Diagram A

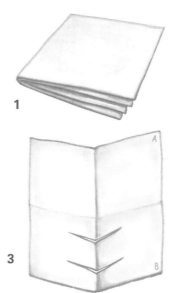

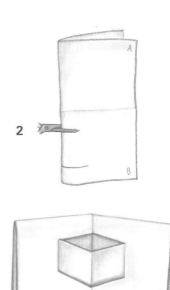

❦ Contemporary Card

Sometimes simple shapes can make the most impressive statement. Add a clever sticker and your greeting is complete.

What you need

5½x11-inch piece of white cardstock
1½-inch colored cardstock squares or
  circles (we used purchased precut shapes)
Glue stick
Purchased 3-D sticker

What you do

Score and fold the white cardstock in half. Arrange squares (or circles) evenly on the front of the card. Use a glue stick to adhere shapes in place.

Place a sticker on the center shape. Write an inside message such as "May Simple Joys Be Yours" or "May Your Christmas be Jolly".

❦ Kitty Tuna Treats

Yes, even your favorite feline deserves a treat for Christmas. Store these yummy tuna treats in made-for-kitty jars.

What you need

Canning jar, top, and ring
Kitty image from old card or magazine
Ribbon, small pompons or jingle bells
Tacky crafts glue
1 recipe Kitty Tuna Treats

What you do

Color-copy or scan and print the desired kitty image. Draw around the jar top on the image and cut out. Glue to jar top. Fill the jar with Kitty Tuna Treats (see recipe, *right*). Place top on jar, then screw ring. Tie jingle bells or glue pompons on the end of ribbon; tie around jar.

Note: Be sure bells or pompons cannot be chewed from ribbon.

Kitty Tuna Treats

1 cup wheat flour
⅓ cup wheat germ
3 tablespoons oatmeal
1 egg
1 tablespoon oil
6-ounce can tuna in oil, undrained

Combine all ingredients in a bowl and mix. Roll out to ¼-inch thickness. Cut into small fish shapes and place on an ungreased cookie sheet. Bake in a 350°F oven for 20 minutes or until firm. Remove from cookie sheet. Cool. Keep treats covered in tight container in refrigerator for up to 1 week. Treats are not intended to replace regular food. Use as treats only.

Note: *Not for human consumption—for kitties only!*

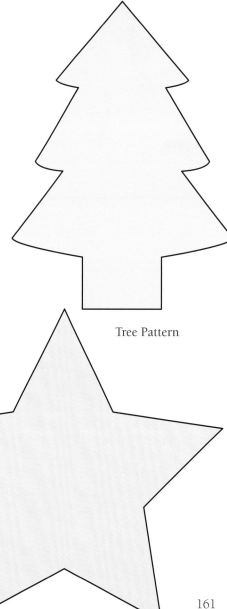

❧ Jeweled Wraps

Let these vintage pins sparkle as they decorate your beautifully wrapped package.

What you need
Vintage jewelry
Wrapped packages without bows
Ribbon to coordinate with the jewelry

What you do
Wrap packages with solid color papers. Decorate with ribbon, leaving the ribbon flat. Pin the jewelry to the ribbon and bows.

❧ Christmas Fun Bags

Simple glittered holiday motifs are added to purchased gift bags for easy wraps.

What you need
Tracing paper
Pencil; scissors
Purchased gift bags

Crafts foam sheets, such as Fun Foam, in desired colors
Round adhesive spacers
Holiday stickers
Tacky crafts glue
Fine glitter

What you do
Trace patterns, *right*, onto tracing paper. Cut out. Trace around the shapes onto crafts foam. Cut out. Decorate with stickers and glitter as desired. Attach the shapes to front of bags using adhesive spacers. Fill with Christmas goodies.

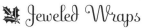

Tree Pattern

Star Pattern

🌿 Quick Wraps

*Pretty ribbons, pretty fabrics, pretty paints—
they all make wraps that make your gift one to
remember.*

What you need

Package to wrap
Scarf; short piece of cording
Old sheet music
Glitter paints in a tube

What you do

For the music wrap, wrap box with
vintage music. Add a line of glitter
between the bars. Tie with a bow.

For the scarf wrap, purchase a holiday
silk scarf and wrap around the box.
Secure in place with a small piece of
cording.

For the painted box, start with a
painted box and make dots with
the glitter paint pen. Spell names or
greetings. The trick to spacing the
names on the boxes is to plan first by
using a pencil to lightly mark the letters
before starting to dot the names.

🌿 Ribbon-Ready Box

*Every gift-giver will love to have a box full of
ribbon all ready for gift wrapping.*

What you need

Large purchased box with lid
*Small purchased box with lid that fits into
  the larger box*
Awl; small washer; crafts glue
*Spools or ribbon in desired colors, prints,
  and styles to put in box*
*Pieces of wide ribbons for decorating
  large box*
7 small purchased ornaments

What you do

To make the small box ribbon dispenser, use the awl to make a hole in the center of the lid of the box. Glue the washer over the hole. Allow to dry. Place a small spool of ribbon in the box and pull the ribbon through the hole. Place the dispenser in the larger box. Surround the dispenser with ribbon on spools in desired colors. Decorate the top of the big box by gluing on wide pieces of ribbon, crisscrossing the ribbon in the center. Glue the ornaments on top of the ribbon. Allow to dry. Put the lid on the box. Add a gift tag if desired.

Soft Felted Purse

Don't throw that old sweater away! Instead, felt it and make a clever purse with matching accessories that will surely be treasured.

What you need

Tracing paper or photocopier
Preshrunk felted sweater
64 inches of ⅜-inch-cording, cut into two 32-inch lengths
½ yard of ¼-inch cording, cut into two 9 inch lengths
Matching thread
¼ heavyweight iron-on interfacing
¼ yard lining fabric

What you do

Trace purse patterns, *pages 164-165*, and cut out. Cut purse pieces from sweater bottom, having top straight edge of pattern aligned with the bottom of the sweater so that the ribbing extends beyond the straight edge. Cut handles from straight grain of remaining sweater fabric, piecing if needed to make two strips 1½x32 inches long and two strips ¾x8 inches long. Cut pocket from sweater front or make one from sweater fabric, using pocket pattern piece. Iron interfacing to wrong sides of purse sweater fabric. With right sides together, sew side and lower edges of purse, starting and

stopping on side edges at the point where the sweater ribbing begins. Use a ¼-inch seam allowance. Clip curves and turn right side out. With wrong sides together, sew remaining side edges of ribbing on purse. Fold ribbing edge to outside of purse. Edgestitch pocket piece to the center of one right side of lining piece, about 1½ inches from top straight edge. With wrong sides together, stitch side and lower edges of lining pieces together, using ¼-inch seam. Fold top edge of lining ½ inch

to wrong side and iron flat. Fold each ¾x8-inch strip of fabric around the ¼-inch cording. Using matching thread, hand stitch long cut edges together around cording. Fold one wrapped cord in half to make a loop and baste in place at center top of back of purse, having cut edges extend ¾ inches into purse from top fold edge of ribbing. With other wrapped narrow cord, tie a loose knot in center as a clasp. Fold in half and baste in place at opposite top edge of purse.

Handmade Gifts and Greetings

Wrap each 32-inch length of ⅜-inch cording with sweater fabric and hand sew long cut edges and each short end of strips. On outside of purse front and back, make small holes to insert handles by clipping slits ¼-inch wide and ⅜-inch long at points marked on pattern, making sure this spot is just under the sweater cuff folded over. Tack the clipped pieces to the backside by taking a few hand stitches.

Tie loose knot in one end of each handle. Insert long straight end of each handle through a hole from the front side of purse then from back side to the outside on the remaining hole. Tie another loose knot near end of handle. Insert other handle through purse in the same manner.

Pin handles to purse at top edges and baste in place at top folded edge, keeping ribbing free. Put lining inside purse, with wrong side of lining facing wrong side of purse. Edgestitch around top edge at fold line, through handles, loop, and knot clasp, laying ribbing out flat. Fold ribbing down to outside of purse to finish.

Tips for Felting Sweaters
Castaway wool sweaters can be recycled into wonderfully tight wool to make all kinds of accessories. Choose sweaters with 100% wool fiber content for best shrinkage. Place the sweater in an old pillowcase to avoid clogging the washer, and wash in very hot water with a small amount of laundry soap. Dry the sweater in a very hot dryer to shrink and "felt" the item to maximum amount. Cut the felted sweater apart and iron between press clothes before using in the project.

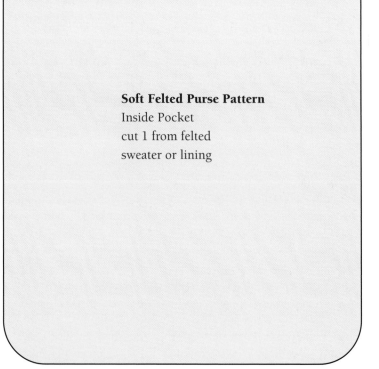

Soft Felted Purse Pattern
Inside Pocket
cut 1 from felted
sweater or lining

Full-size Pattern

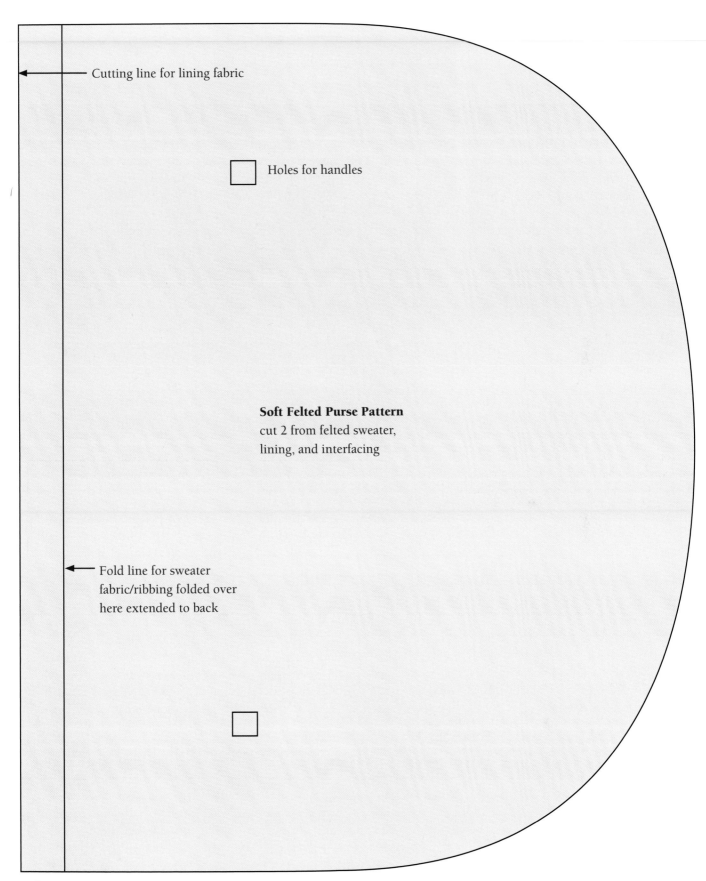

Cutting line for lining fabric

Holes for handles

Soft Felted Purse Pattern
cut 2 from felted sweater,
lining, and interfacing

Fold line for sweater
fabric/ribbing folded over
here extended to back

Full-size pattern

🌿 Pretty Ribbon-Trimmed Cards

Rubber stamp your favorite message and then add purchased stickers and a piece of your favorite ribbon. So easy to make, these cards can be sent to everyone on your Christmas list.

What you need

Purchased teal blue blank greeting cards
Rubber stamp with Christmas greeting
Red ink pad
Fine red glitter
Small round and square stickers
Small pieces of 1-inch-wide printed ribbon
Clear crafts glue

What you do

Stamp the greeting on the front of the cards using the rubber stamp and ink pad. Dust with glitter. Let dry. Glue the ribbon to the edge or top of the card. Add the stickers where desired.

🌿 Fleecy Winter Wear

So easy to make and so fun to give, the mittens in this fleece set of winter wear are tucked away in a jar.

What you need

Tracing paper
1 yard of 45-inch-wide fleece
⅜-inch wide clear elastic—for small, 12 inches of elastic (two 6-inch pieces)—for large, 18 inches of elastic (two 9-inch pieces)
Matching thread
Pinking shears
Scissors
Canning jar; curly ribbon

What you do

For mittens, enlarge desired pattern, *opposite,* onto tracing paper. Cut out. Use pinking shears to cut 4 mitten patterns, placing stretch to go around hand. Using ¼-inch seams and right

sides together, sew mitten pieces together from notch to bottom edge. Open up mitten. On the wrong side, mark a line for elastic placement, 2½ inches up from bottom edge. Cut elastic to length needed leaving 1-inch from end to hold on to under presser foot to make it easier to stretch across the mitten. Stretching elastic, zigzag over the elastic and sew in place. With right sides together, sew mitten from notch around to lower edge, matching elastic marks. Repeat for other mitten. Turn right side out. *For scarf,* cut fleece into a rectangle 8½-inches wide and 45 inches long. Use pinking shears to cut fringe on each end of fleece cutting every ½ inch in to a depth of 3 inches. *For the mitten wrap,* cut out desired art and use as tags and jar inset. Roll mittens and put in jar. Tie tags on with curly ribbon.

Large and Small Mitten Patterns

Enlarge 200%

🎄 Joyous Noel Card

Greet everyone on your Christmas card list with this clever winter scene sending a holiday message.

What you need

Tracing paper
Scissors
1x2-inch rectangular art gum eraser (available at office and art stores)
Pencil
Sharp knife
One 5x12-inch piece of blue cardstock
Light blue rubber stamp ink pad
Fine light blue glitter
Metal dimensional alphabet square stickers (available at scrapbooking stores)

What you do

Trace the tree pattern, *below*, onto tracing paper. Cut out and draw around the tree onto the front of the eraser. The edges of the tree should just touch the eraser edges. Cut out around the edges with a sharp knife, leaving a raised portion that is in the shape of the tree. Make a few cuts into the tree for texture. Score the cardstock and fold in half. Press the stamp into the ink pad and make tree shapes across the bottom of the card. Using your finger, make a few small fingerprints across the card front. Dust with glitter while still wet. Let dry. Position the letters to spell NOEL on the top of the card.

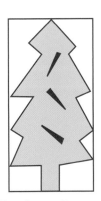

Tree Stamp Pattern

167

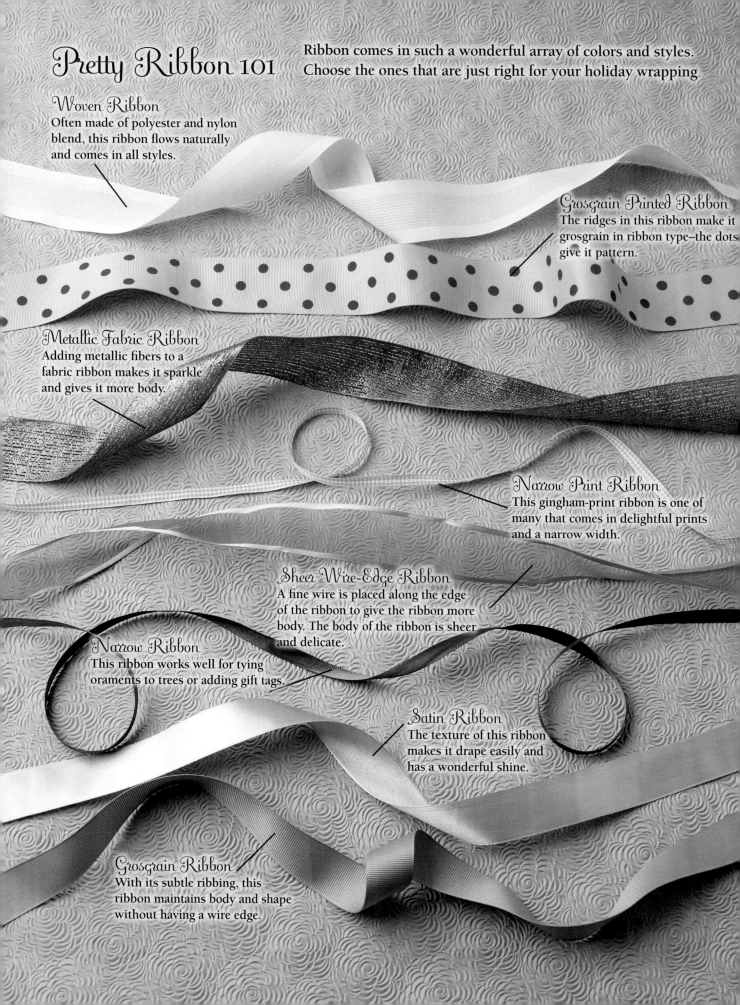

Pretty Ribbon 101

Ribbon comes in such a wonderful array of colors and styles. Choose the ones that are just right for your holiday wrapping.

Woven Ribbon
Often made of polyester and nylon blend, this ribbon flows naturally and comes in all styles.

Grosgrain Printed Ribbon
The ridges in this ribbon make it grosgrain in ribbon type–the dots give it pattern.

Metallic Fabric Ribbon
Adding metallic fibers to a fabric ribbon makes it sparkle and gives it more body.

Narrow Print Ribbon
This gingham-print ribbon is one of many that comes in delightful prints and a narrow width.

Sheer Wire-Edge Ribbon
A fine wire is placed along the edge of the ribbon to give the ribbon more body. The body of the ribbon is sheer and delicate.

Narrow Ribbon
This ribbon works well for tying oraments to trees or adding gift tags.

Satin Ribbon
The texture of this ribbon makes it drape easily and has a wonderful shine.

Grosgrain Ribbon
With its subtle ribbing, this ribbon maintains body and shape without having a wire edge.

More Ideas

To add a little sparkle to your handmade gift, make a simple tag using purchased scrapbook tags. Use rhinestone alphabet stickers to spell the name of the lucky person who is receiving the gift.

Make a "choose-a-gift" centerpiece by wrapping tiny gifts and placing them in a large bowl in the center of the table. Let everyone choose a gift for a table favor.

Old photos make wonderful images on the front of greeting cards. Color-copy the photos and adhere to the front of a folded piece of cardstock. Don't be afraid to use the ones that feature you as a teenager!

Purchase a simple greeting card and make it your own by adding a bit of glue and glitter to solid areas of color. Sign your name using a glitter pen and write "sparkle added by _____."

To make a clever card for giving money, use decorative scissors to cut off the top of a small colored envelope. Decorate it with metallic markers. Glue it to the front of your blank card. Fold the money and slide it inside the envelope pocket.

Go to the movie theater and buy an empty popcorn box. Fill the box with a favorite DVD, a bag of microwave popcorn, seasoning salt, special candies, and napkins. Add a tag that says, "Join me for a movie?"

Use the fronts of old Christmas cards to cut into puzzle pieces. Put the pieces into a colorful envelope and take along for a "something to do" gift for the kids while you drive to the mall to go Christmas shopping.

Make a gift that has a child's touch. Choose a colorful flat front picture frame. Pour a little acrylic paint on a plate and let the kids dip their fingers in the paint and make fingerprints on the frame. Let it dry and place a picture of the kids in the frame.

A plain votive candle holder is easy to dress up with just a little glitter. Make designs on the glass using white crafts glue and dust with glitter. Allow to dry. Place a candle in the votive for a sparkling gift.

Purchase a holiday towel at a linen or discount store. Choose holiday soaps and tube of hand lotion that match the colors of the towel. Roll the soaps and the lotion in the towel and tie with a pretty ribbon.

Use the kid's extra artwork to wrap Grandma's package this year. She'll save the wrapping!

Make gift-making a family affair. Gather together mom, dad, grandma, grandpa, and the kids to pop some popcorn, play a game, and make handmade gifts.

Use a starched baby stocking as a gift-holder for money and hang on the tree.

Soup Suppers
and
Holiday Breads

Spend a winter night Christmas

caroling and then come in from

the cold for a flavor-filled bowl of

steaming soup and homemade bread.

You'll find the best soups, breads,

and rolls in this chapter to make your

holiday oh-so-cozy.

Everyone's winter favorite, **Old-Fashioned Chicken and Noodles**, is the perfect Christmas Eve meal. So rich and hearty it will become a holiday tradition. Pretty red potatoes and green parsley make **Parsley Potato Soup** a holiday meal with the colors of the season. Serve with crackers or muffins for a complete meal. Make Christmas morning extra special with a **Breakfast Sausage Roll** that is made the night before and baked that morning. Serve sweet **Carrot-Pecan Muffins** with any favorite soup. Wrap up a **Frosted Orange Roll** for a much-loved gift. Recipes start on page 186. The Frosted Orange Roll recipe is on page193.

F Filled with all the goodness that a potato soup should have—potatoes, vegetables, and a creamy broth, **Hearty Red Potato Soup** is quick to make and happily satisfies everyone at the table.

Heart healthy **Minestrone Soup** starts with a tomato base and is filled with favorite vegetables and pasta. Use a pretty bow-tie pasta or even a holiday motif pasta to make the soup even more festive. Delicious with any soup or for a holiday treat anytime, **Lemon Poppy Seed Muffins** have a wonderful flavor and texture with a hint of lemon zest and poppy seeds. Recipes start on page 188.

A sweet beginning to any day, serve everyone at the table a **Christmas Morning Sticky Roll** and there will be smiles all around. The rolls are a sweet yeast bread with dried cherries rolled into the batter before slicing.

So simple to make—stir up a batch of **Family Favorite Chili** for a big crowd at holiday time. Using canned tomatoes makes the chili quick and economical, yet delightfully filling. Recipes start on page 190.

Soup Suppers and Holiday Breads

Sure to be asked for all year long, **Aunt Lizzy's Banana Bread** is easy to make. The secret to its light texture is the buttermilk in the recipe.

You can have plenty of **Heart Healthy Muffins** because they are filled with ingredients that are especially good for you—oatmeal, cranberries, canola oil—and yes, they taste so very good.

Make a big pot of **Vegetable Beef Soup** to have on hand when they come in from sledding. The rich beef broth and vegetables will hit the spot! Recipes start on page191.

So sweet and creamy, **Fresh Corn Chowder** is a healthy soup to serve during the cold winter months. Serve it after Christmas caroling with crackers and cheese. With just a hint of orange zest for an unexpected and delightful flavor, **Frosted Orange Rolls** make a welcome addition to any meal. **Tomato Bisque and Crispy Rice Crackers** are a great combination. The soup is quick to make using canned tomatoes and the crackers use crunchy rice cereal. Recipes start on page 193.

Drizzled with powdered sugar frosting, **Spiced Pumpkin Loaves** make great last minute gifts that everyone will love—but be sure to keep plenty on hand for holiday guests as well. The combination of sweet oranges and tart cranberries make **Orange Cranberry Muffins** a favorite any time of year. Serve them during the holidays with a favorite soup or casserole. Beautifully rich, **Wild Rice and Mushroom Soup** is filled with colorful shedded carrots and sliced mushrooms that accent the lovely wild-rice texture. Recipes start on page 194.

They'll love to come in from the cold for a hot cup of **Tomato Basil Soup and Cheesy Biscuits**. The soup is made with just a few ingredients so it cooks up in no time. Make Christmas morning even more special with homemade bread that you make yourself. Rolled out just like cinnamon rolls, these **Caramel Pecan Pull-Aparts** have a pecan and brown sugar topping. The recipes start on page 196.

Parsley Potato Soup

In this soup the potatoes are cooked first and then added to the parsley-flavored white sauce base. Chunks of ham make the soup hearty and oh-so-tasty.

Old-Fashioned Chicken and Noodles

Thick and rich and full of flavor, this old time dish will become one that is asked for every year. Let the children help make the noodles.

What you need

1 whole chicken
Water to cover chicken
1 teaspoon salt
½ cup celery, chopped
1 small onion, chopped

What you need for the noodles

2 cups all-purpose flour
1 teaspoon salt
1 egg
3 egg yolks
¼–½ cups water

What you do

Wash the chicken and cut up into pieces. Place in large pan on stove and cover with water. Add salt, celery, and onion, and cook until tender, about 30 minutes. Remove the chicken from the bone, cut up, cover, and set aside in refrigerator. Strain broth and set aside.

To make the noodles, mix the flour and salt and place in a large bowl. Set aside. Beat the egg and add the egg yolks and water, mixing well. With a spoon make a well in the center of the dry ingredients. Add the eggs and water mixture. Mix until it forms a ball and knead until smooth.

Dust the rolling surface with flour. With a rolling pin, roll the dough into a rectangle about ¼-inch thick. Cut into ⅛-inch strips for narrow noodles or ¼-inch strips for wider noodles. Shake noodles out after cutting and place on a floured cookie sheet. Set aside.

Bring the broth to a boil in a crock pot or large pan. Add the noodles; cook until tender, about 4 hours in slow cooker on high or about 20 minutes on the stove. Add the cut-up chicken. Makes about 8 servings.

What you need

4 cups chicken or turkey broth
2 cups chopped parsley (no stems)
½ cup chopped onion
1 teaspoon sugar
½ teaspoon salt
2 tablespoons butter
2 cups milk
¼ cup all-purpose flour
2 cups cubed or sliced cooked potatoes
½ cup cubed ham
Pepper to taste

What you do

In a large saucepan combine the broth, parsley, onion, sugar, and salt. Simmer for 30 minutes. Remove from heat and strain. Return strained liquid to saucepan. Discard solids from strainer. In a small saucepan melt the butter. Stir in the flour and milk. Cook for about 3 minutes or until thick and creamy, stirring constantly. Add the milk mixture to the strained broth. Bring just to a boil. Reduce heat and add the potatoes and cubed ham. Heat

until very hot (do not boil) and serve immediately. Garnish with fresh parsley. Makes 6 servings.

Breakfast Sausage Roll

Filled with hearty sausage, mushrooms, and cheese, this make-ahead treat is a breakfast rolled up all in one. Sliced and served with fruit or juice, this delicious roll is the perfect Christmas breakfast.

What you need

2 loaves purchased frozen bread
1 pound Italian sausage
1 pound hamburger
1 cup broccoli, chopped
1½ cups mozzarella cheese, shredded
½ cup mushrooms, sliced

What you do

Thaw bread and roll out each loaf to a 9x11-inch rectangle. Brown meat and drain. Add broccoli, cheese, and mushrooms. Spread half of the mixture on each rolled out rectangle. Roll up from the long side and seal the edges by pinching them together. Place each loaf on a greased cookie sheet and let rise about 1 hour. Bake in a 325°F oven for about 35 minutes. Each loaf makes about 6 servings. To freeze, place on greased cookie sheet, cover and freeze

immediately. When ready to bake, thaw in refrigerator overnight. Let rise, and bake as directed.

Carrot-Pecan Muffins

Spicy and sweet, these muffins are sure to please everyone at the table. Shredded fresh carrots, pineapple, and pecans combine with just the right spices to make these a traditional favorite.

What you need

2 eggs
1¼ cups freshly shredded carrots
¾ cup sugar
½ cup vegetable oil
½ cup buttermilk
½ cup crushed pineapple, drained
⅔ cup pecans
2 ¼ cups all-purpose flour
1 teaspoon baking soda
2 teaspoons baking powder
1 teaspoon ground cinnamon
¼ teaspoon ground nutmeg
¼ teaspoon ground cloves
1 teaspoon vanilla

What you do

In a medium mixing bowl beat the eggs. Add the carrots, sugar, oil, buttermilk, pineapple, and pecans. Mix well.

Set aside. In a large mixing bowl, stir together the flour, soda, baking powder, and spices. Add the carrot mixture to the dry ingredients and blend well. Add the vanilla. Do not overmix.

Pour into greased 12-cup muffin pan. Place pecan half on top of each muffin. Bake in a 375°F oven for about 15 minutes or until toothpick comes out clean. Refrigerate any leftover muffins. Makes 12 muffins.

Note: Using prepackaged shredded carrots may cause discoloration in finished muffin.

🍂 Hearty Red Potato Soup

Choose pretty red potatoes for this creamy soup to make a colorful presentation.

What you need

2 cups cooked and cubed red-skin potatoes
1 tablespoon butter
¼ cup chopped red pepper
¼ cup chopped green pepper
¼ cup chopped celery
¼ cup chopped onion
1 tablespoon flour
½ cup milk
1 cup chicken broth
¾ cup frozen or fresh peas
1 cup milk
1 cup light cream
Salt and pepper to taste

What you do

Note: Be sure to cook potatoes in boiling water with skins on. Drain and set aside.

In a heavy saucepan, melt the butter. Sauté red pepper, green pepper, celery, and onion. Combine flour with the ½ cup milk. Add to the vegetables in the saucepan. Cook until thickened.

Add chicken broth and peas and bring to a boil. Boil 1 minute. Add the 1 cup milk and cream. Heat, but do not boil. Cube or slice cooked potatoes and add to mixture. Add salt and pepper, and serve immediately. Serves 8.

🍂 Minestrone Soup

Pretty and chock full of vegetables, this soup is full of color and flavor.

What you need

1 tablespoon olive oil
1 small onion
¼ cup celery, diced
¼ cup red bell pepper, chopped
¼ cup green bell pepper, chopped
⅛ teaspoon each of oregano, basil, garlic, and pepper
½ teaspoon of dried parsley
1 teaspoon salt
1 can beef broth (14.5 oz.)
1 can chicken broth (14.5 oz.)
½ cup fresh broccoli florets
½ cup fresh green beans, cut up
½ cup carrots, sliced
1 can diced tomatoes (14.5 oz.)
1 cup uncooked bow-tie pasta
Parmesan cheese, shredded

What you do

Preheat oven to 400°F. Grease bottoms of medium-sized muffin pan. In a large bowl beat eggs and milk and stir in oil. In another large bowl, mix flour and poppy seeds together. Stir in all other ingredients. Add egg, milk, oil mixture and mix until just blended. Do not overmix. Batter should be lumpy.

Fill muffin cups ¾ full. Bake for about 15 minutes or until golden brown. Makes 12 muffins.

Lemon Powdered Sugar Glaze

Stir together 3 tablespoons lemon juice and 1 cup powdered sugar until smooth. Drizzle over the top of each muffin and sprinkle with coarse white sugar.

What you do

In large saucepan, saute onion, celery, and peppers in oil. Add spices, salt, and pepper. Add beef and chicken broth. Cook over low heat until boiling. Let simmer 10 more minutes.

Steam broccoli, beans, and carrots until tender. Add vegetables and canned tomatoes to broth. Bring to boil.

Add pasta to the boiling broth mixture. Cook until pasta becomes tender, about 8 minutes. Serve with shredded parmesan cheese. Makes about 6 servings.

Lemon Poppy Seed Muffins

Lemon Poppy Seed Muffins are sure to be a hit any time of year, but at the holidays they taste even better. Top them off with a powdered sugar glaze and sprinkle with coarse white sugar.

What you need

2 eggs
1 cup whole milk
¼ cup canola oil
2 tablespoons poppy seeds
⅓ cup sugar
3 teaspoons baking powder
½ teaspoon salt
1 tablespoon grated lemon rind
2¼ cups all-purpose flour

Special Tip

Zest is the outside skin of a citrus fruit such as a lemon or orange. To create the zest, or grated citrus skin, the washed fruit is rubbed or grated over a small grater or zester. By making tiny pieces of the skin, the flavor and aroma is released. Use your favorite zest in cookies, breads, or any where you want to add a lovely citrus flavor.

Christmas Morning Sticky Rolls

They'll be all smiles when you present them with this all-time favorite breakfast treat

What you need

1 cup packed brown sugar
¼ cup butter, melted
¼ cup light corn syrup
¼ cup light cream
2 cups warm water
2 packages dry yeast
½ cup butter, melted
⅓ cup sugar
1 tablespoon salt
1 egg
6 to 6½ cups flour
½ cup dried cherries

What you do

Grease a 9x13-inch cake pan. Combine the first four ingredients, pour into bottom of pan. Set aside.

Put warm water into large mixing bowl. Dissolve yeast in water. Add ½ cup butter, sugar, and salt. Beat egg and add to mixture. Add 2 cups of the flour, beat thoroughly. Let rest for five minutes. Gradually add remaining flour and mix. Turn out onto floured surface and knead until smooth. Place dough back in bowl. Cover and let rise until double in bulk.

Roll out dough into 12x16-inch rectangle. Spread with a mixture of ½ cup softened butter, ¾ cup sugar and 1 tablespoon cinnamon. Add dried cherries. Roll up and slice 1½ inches thick and lay in prepared cake pan. Bake in a 350°F oven for about 30 minute, or until bubbly and brown. Invert onto foil. Cool slightly before serving. Decorate with candied cherries if desired. Makes about 16 large rolls.

❧ Family Favorite Chili

Come in from the cold and warm up with some piping hot chili. Serve with cheese and crackers or wheat rolls and honey butter.

What you need

1 small onion, chopped
1 small red pepper, chopped
1 small green pepper, chopped
2 tablespoons olive oil
2 pounds lean ground beef
2 cans diced tomatoes (14.5 oz.)
1 can whole tomatoes (14.5 oz.)
1 can crushed tomatoes (28 oz.)
1 can chili beans (14.5 oz.)
2 teaspoons chili powder
1 teaspoon minced garlic
1 teaspoon black pepper
½ teaspoon salt
Star pasta and sliced cheese (optional)

What you do

In a large saucepan, sauté onions and peppers in the olive oil. Add ground beef and cook thoroughly. Drain well. Add tomatoes, beans, and seasonings. Cook until bubbly. Continue cooking on low heat, stirring often for 30 minutes. If cooking in a slow cooker, transfer cooked onion, peppers, and ground beef to crock pot. Add all other ingredients. Cook on high heat for 4 to 5 hours. Makes about 8 large servings. Garnish with star pasta and slices of cheese if desired.

Heart-Healthy Muffins

Please your palate and your body, too, with these tasty and good-for-you hearty oatmeal muffins.

What you need

2 ¼ cups flour
2 cups oatmeal
⅔ cup sugar
2 teaspoons baking powder
½ teaspoon soda
¼ teaspoon salt
⅓ cup dried cranberries
⅓ cup canola oil
1 whole egg plus 1 egg white
1 cup buttermilk
¼ cup favorite jam

Oatmeal Topping

3 tablespoons sugar
1 teaspoon cinnamon
3 tablespoons oatmeal
1 tablespoon canola oil

What you do

In a large bowl, mix dry ingredients and dried cranberries. In a small bowl, whip oil, eggs and buttermilk. Make a well in dry ingredients and add oil mixture. Mix until just combined. Do not overmix. Spoon into greased muffin cups, filling about ¾ full.

Make an indentation in the center of each muffin and add 1 tablespoon

Aunt Lizzy's Banana Bread

An old-time favorite, these golden loaves of rich banana flavor make great gifts.

What you need

1 cup sugar
½ cup butter, softened
2 eggs
3 ripe bananas, mashed
1 teaspoon baking powder
1 teaspoon baking soda
¼ teaspoon salt
3 tablespoons buttermilk
2 cups flour

What you do

In a mixing bowl, cream sugar and butter, add eggs and mashed bananas. Mix baking powder, baking soda, and salt with the buttermilk and add to the

creamed mixture. Stir together. Add the 2 cups flour and mix well. Pour into 2 well-greased 7½x4x2¾-inch loaf pans and bake in a 350°F oven for 25 minutes or until a toothpick comes out clean. Drizzle with Powdered Sugar Frosting and sprinkle with red sugar.

Powdered Sugar Frosting
In a bowl, mix 2 cups sifted powdered sugar, 2 tablespoons milk, and 1 tablespoon melted butter together until well blended.

What you do

To make the beef stock, place the shanks or soup bone in a large stock pot and cover with water. Add the onion, celery, salt, and pepper. Bring to a boil. Reduce heat. Cover and simmer for about 1½ hours or until the meat is tender and falling off the bones.

Remove bones and meat from stock pot and place on plate or in bowl. Remove meat from bones, cover, and place in refrigerator until ready to use. Strain broth into bowl and cool in refrigerator. Skim off fat.

Place broth into large saucepan. Add carrots and sweet potatoes. Bring to a boil. Cover and simmer about 15 minutes or until tender.

Add the other vegetables, meat, and more salt and pepper to taste if desired. Bring to a boil. Simmer 5 more minutes or until vegetables are tender. Serve immediately. Makes 8 servings.

Special Tip

Any soup that contains a variety of vegetables is always a treat. But to manage to keep the vegetables all cooked to a perfect consistency can be tricky. The secret to keeping the vegetables all crisp and not overcooked is to add the vegetables to the soup or stew at different times. Add the carrots and other firm vegetables first. Then add potatoes, and fresh green beans. Last, add any small or leafy vegetables such as corn, peas, or shredded cabbage. Your vegetables will all be perfectly tender at the same time.

of jam. Mix all ingredients for Oatmeal Topping and sprinkle on tops of muffins. Bake in a 400°F oven for 15 minutes or until muffins are lightly browned. Makes 12 muffins.

Vegetable Beef Soup

A rich vegetable soup is always a welcome meal after being outside in the winter cold. This soup offers wonderful flavor and healthy, colorful vegetables. Sweet potatoes, small pieces of red cabbage, sliced carrots, and bright green peas make this meal a favorite.

What you need

3 pounds beef shanks or 1 large soup bone
1 quart water
1 medium onion, chopped
½ cup celery, chopped
1 teaspoon salt
1 teaspoon pepper
1 cup sliced carrots
1 cup diced sweet potatoes
½ cup each frozen corn, peas, and green beans
¼ cup chopped red cabbage

❧ Fresh Corn Chowder

Perfect for cold winter nights, this fresh corn chowder warms the heart and soul with its creamy milk base and colorful vegetables.

What you need

2 tablespoons butter
1 small onion, chopped
¼ cup carrots, diced
¼ cup celery, chopped
¼ cup red and green peppers, diced
2 tablespoons flour
1 teaspoon salt
1 teaspoon pepper
1 can chicken broth (14 oz.)
1 cup fresh or frozen corn
¾ cup cream
1 cup milk

What you do

Melt butter in heavy saucepan. Sauté onion, carrots, celery, and red and green peppers in the butter. Set aside. Mix flour, salt, pepper and chicken broth together. Add to vegetables and bring to a boil. If using fresh corn, cook on the cob and drain. Slice off the cob. Add fresh or frozen corn, cream, and milk to soup mixture. Heat thoroughly without boiling. Simmer until ready to serve. Makes about 6 servings.

Frosted Orange Rolls

Grated orange rind is the secret to these delicious sweet rolls drizzled with orange juice frosting. Make each roll just a little larger than usual and the smiles will last all day long. For a quick Christmas morning gift for a favorite neighbor, place the roll on a small plate and wrap with a piece of clear cellophane and a pretty red bow.

What you need

⅓ cup sugar
1 teaspoon salt
⅓ cup butter
1 cup scalded milk
1 package of dry yeast
¼ cup warm water
1 egg, beaten
3 tablespoons grated orange rind
4 cups all-purpose flour
1 recipe Orange Frosting

What you do

Place sugar, salt, and butter in pan. Add milk. Heat and stir until butter is melted. Dissolve yeast in the warm water in a 2-quart bowl. Add cooled milk mixture, beaten egg, and orange rind. Add flour to form a stiff dough. Turn out and knead until smooth and elastic, about 5 minutes, using more flour if necessary. Place in bowl; let rise until doubled. Punch down and roll into a 9x13-inch rectangle. Spread with ¼ cup butter, ¼ cup sugar, 1 teaspoon cinnamon. Roll up and slice into 1½-inch slices. Place in greased muffin tin. Let rise for 45 minutes. Bake in a 350°F oven for 20 minutes or until brown. Cool. Drizzle with Orange Frosting. Makes 16 rolls. Can be frozen for up to 3 weeks.

Orange Frosting

In a bowl, mix 1 tablespoon butter, 1 cup powdered sugar, and 2 tablespoons orange juice. Beat until smooth.

Spiced Pumpkin Loaves

Ready to slice on Christmas morning, this pumpkin bread is full of sugar and spice. Make extra to freeze and serve or give to friends that come to wish you a Merry Christmas.

What you need

3⅓ cups all-purpose flour
3 cups sugar
2 teaspoons baking soda
1½ teaspoons salt
1 teaspoon nutmeg
1 teaspoon cinnamon
¼ teaspoon cloves
1 cup vegetable oil
4 eggs
⅔ cup water
2 cups canned pumpkin
1 recipe Frosting Glaze

What you do

Sift all dry ingredients together. Add the oil, eggs, water, and pumpkin to the dry ingredients. Mix well and pour into 3 large greased bread pans. Bake in a 350°F oven for 1 hour. Cool. Makes 3 loaves. Drizzle loaves with frosting. Garnish with candied cherries.

> **Frosting Glaze**
> In a bowl, mix 1 cup sifted powdered sugar and 1 tablespoon milk. Beat together until well blended.

Tomato Bisque and Crispy Rice Crackers

Perfect for a soup supper after Christmas caroling, this tangy soup will become a yearly tradition.

What you need for the soup

2 tablespoons butter
2 tablespoons flour
14 oz. can chicken broth
2 cups vegetable juice, such as V8
1 large can (1 lb. 4 oz.) diced tomatoes
2 tablespoons snipped fresh basil or 1 teaspoon dried basil, crushed
Salt and pepper to taste
Sour cream

What you need for crackers

1 cup butter
2 cups flour
2 cups shredded cheddar cheese
2 cups crisp rice cereal

What you do for the soup

In a large heavy saucepan, melt the butter. Stir in the flour until blended. Add the chicken broth. Simmer until thick. Add the vegetable juice, diced tomatoes, basil, salt, and pepper. Simmer until ready to eat. Garnish with sour cream. Serves 6.

To make the monogram letter, place cold sour cream into a decorator bag. Pipe the monogram on the soup just before serving.

What you do for the crackers

In a small bowl, beat the butter and the flour. Add the shredded cheese and rice cereal. Mix well. Form into 1-inch balls.

Place the balls on a greased cookie sheet. Flatten the balls with a damp fork. Bake in a 325°F oven for about 20 minutes. Remove from oven and cool on wire rack. Makes about 3 dozen crackers.

🎄 Orange Cranberry Muffins

Cuddle up with your favorite book, a Christmas carol, and a warm Orange Cranberry Muffin to make a holiday evening complete.

What you need

2 eggs
1 ½ cups buttermilk
⅓ cup canola oil
2 ½ cups all-purpose flour
⅓ cup sugar
2 teaspoons baking powder
½ teaspoon baking soda
½ teaspoon salt
1 tablespoon grated orange rind
¾ cup dried cranberries

Topping

3 tablespoons yellow decorator sugar
1 teaspoon ground cinnamon

What you do

Grease bottoms of medium-sized muffin cup pan. Beat eggs and milk and stir in oil. Stir in all other ingredients and mix until just blended. Batter should be lumpy. Do not overmix. Fill muffin cups ¾ full. Mix sugar and cinnamon together and sprinkle a little of the mixture on top of each muffin. Bake in a 400°F oven for about 15 minutes or until golden brown. Makes 12 muffins.

Special Tip

To make perfect muffins every time, remember that muffins, unlike cakes, need to be mixed only until the dry and liquid ingredients have been blended. Muffins are best when made by hand with the least amount of mixing, just enough to be sure all ingredients are blended, but never beaten. This will avoid having holes or "tunnels" in the finished muffin.

Wild Rice and Mushroom Soup

Steamy and hot and filled with all kinds of healthy goodness, this soup is quick to make and oh-so-delicious.

What you need

2 tablespoons butter
2 tablespoons green onions, chopped
¼ cup shredded carrots
¼ cup flour
4 cups chicken broth
2 cups cooked and drained wild rice
⅔ cup sliced fresh mushrooms
1 cup half and half
Salt and pepper

What you do

Melt the butter in a heavy saucepan. Cook the green onions and carrots in the hot butter. Add the flour and mix well. Pour in the chicken broth and bring to a boil. Boil one minute. Add the wild rice, mushrooms, and half and half. Add salt and pepper to taste. Heat but do not boil. Serve immediately. Makes 6 servings.

Tomato Basil Soup and Cheesy Biscuits

Perfect for a soup supper after Christmas caroling, this tangy soup will become a yearly tradition. Serve with star-shaped cheesy biscuits.

What you need for the soup

1 tablespoon butter
¼ cup chopped onion
¼ teaspoon dried thyme
2 teaspoons dried basil
2 tablespoons all-purpose flour
2 cups chicken broth
4 cups canned diced tomatoes
¼ cup light cream
Salt and pepper to taste
2 slices bacon, cooked and crumbled

What you need for the biscuits

2 ¼ cups biscuit mix
⅔ cups milk or as directed on biscuit
* mix box*
½ cup shredded cheddar cheese
Star-shaped cookie cutter

What you do for the soup

In a large saucepan, cook onions in butter until tender. Stir in the flour, thyme, and basil. Add chicken broth and tomatoes and bring to a boil, stirring constantly. Cover and simmer for 10 minutes. Remove from heat. Add cream to soup mixture, return to heat and heat to simmer. Do not boil. Remove from heat, ladle into bowls or cups and sprinkle with bacon pieces. Makes 6 servings.

What you do for the biscuits

Mix biscuit dough as directed on package. Add shredded cheese. Roll out to ½-inch thick. Cut with star cookie cutter. Place on ungreased cookie sheet. Bake in a 400°F oven for 10 minutes or until golden brown. Serve biscuits immediately. Makes 10 biscuits.

Caramel Pecan Pull-Aparts

They'll ask for more when they taste these oh-so-light rolls filled with cinnamon and sugar and covered with caramel and pecans.

What you need

½ cup milk
1 cup lukewarm water
½ cup dry milk
2 packages dry yeast
1 tablespoon sugar
¾ cup shortening
¾ cup sugar
2 teaspoons salt
2 eggs, beaten
6–7 cups all-purpose flour
¾ cup pecan halves

What you do

Mix the milk, water, dry milk, yeast, and 1 tablespoon sugar together in a bowl. Set aside. Melt the shortening. Allow to cool. Add the ¾ cup sugar, shortening, salt, and beaten eggs to the yeast mixture.

Beat in the flour until it is stiff. Turn out on floured board and knead until smooth and elastic. Set in large bowl and cover with damp towel. Let rise for about an hour or until double in bulk. Punch down and roll half of the dough out into a 9x13-inch rectangle shape.

Spread with ¼ cup butter, ¼ cup brown sugar, ¼ cup white sugar, and 1 teaspoon cinnamon. Roll up and slice into 1½-inch slices.

In the bottom of an 8x8-inch pan, mix ¼ cup melted butter, ¼ cup brown sugar, and 1 tablespoon corn syrup.

Lay pecans upside down in butter mixture. Lay the rolls in pan over the mixture. Repeat for other half of dough. Cover and let rise for 30 minutes. Bake in a 350°F oven for about 25 minutes. Remove from oven and turn upside down onto foil. Makes 18 rolls.

Soup Garnishes 101

Simple, and sometimes unexpected, toppings make any soup prettier and healthier.

Chopped Onions
Fresh green onions work the best for a quick soup topper—chop them very fine.

Salad Croutons
Croutons aren't just for salads— they add a wonderful flavor and texture to most any soup.

Shredded Cheese
Any cheese that shreds well makes a great topper—try cheddar, swiss, or mozzarella.

Shredded Carrots
Add a touch of freshness and crunch with a few freshly shredded carrots.

Chopped Parsley
Add color and flavor to any soup with a sprig of pretty green parsley.

Homemade Star Toppers
Use a small star cutter to cut out little star shapes from purchased ready-to-bake biscuits.

Cooked Bacon
The hint of a hickory smoke flavor makes tiny pieces of bacon a great topping for potato or tomato soups.

Blue Cheese Crumbles
Purchase these little flavor treats in small containers at your grocery store. They come already crumbled and ready to serve.

More Ideas

Have the whole family help make quick breads for holiday meals and gifts. For banana bread, let the children mash the bananas on a plate using a dinner fork. This is a great way to get the little ones interested in cooking with you in the kitchen—and they really do help with the preparation of the bread!

For a soup supper, tuck silverware into a purchased mitten and lay beside a steaming bowl of soup.

When presenting your holiday dishes this year, don't forget the garnishes on the serving platters. Use thin slices of lemon, sprigs of fresh mint, sliced apples, pretty carrot curls, or a strip of twisted orange rind to garnish the lovely platters and plates that hold your special recipes.

Using large cookie cutters, cut bread into holiday shapes before making French toast for Christmas morning breakfast. Serve raspberry syrup and red jellies and jams with this fun-shaped favorite toast to make the breakfast complete.

On Christmas Eve, host a soup potluck. Have everyone bring there favorite soup in a slow cooker. You furnish the bread and cheese. This easy supper is sure to become a tradition that everyone looks forward to.

Before doing your holiday grocery shopping, ask each member of the family to choose a favorite recipe to make during the holidays. Be sure to include the ingredients on your shopping list.

To spend as much time as possible with family and friends during the holidays, do your baking ahead of time. Select recipes that can be baked and frozen to serve at a later date.

When doing your holiday shopping, stock up on food containers that are on sale or have a Christmas theme. They will come in handy when you want to send goodies home with your guests.

During the holidays, remember to keep healthy snacks on hand. Carrots, grapes, celery, and other bite-size fruits and veggies make a great last-minute snack.

Be creative when you are serving your soup and chowders. Choose uniquely shaped bowls, large cups, and small pedestal bowls to present your favorite soup recipes.

Add a touch of color and flavor to almost any muffin recipe. Before the muffin is baked, drop a teaspoon of your favorite jelly in the center of the unbaked batter in each muffin cup. The jelly will bake into the muffin for a delightful surprise.

Decorating All Through the House

From the front door to the mantel—from the banister to the windows—make every part of your holiday home sing with the joys of the season.

Use colorful retro fabric to make simple **Vintage Christmas Stockings**. Transparent stickers and glitter dress up **Sparkling Holiday Frames** in no time. Green cardstock holly leaves and red jingle bells gather together to make a cheery **Paper Holly Wreath**. A favorite punch technique is used to create a **Merry Christmas Lampshade**. Bright holiday fabric and purchased fringe trim combine to make **Happy Holiday Stockings**. Fill a simple basket with candy canes and holiday trims for a **Candy Cane Greeting**. Instructions start on page 218. The Vintage Christmas Stocking instructions are on page 226.

Providing beauty and lovely aroma, **Citrus Pomanders** are an age-old Christmas decoration. The fruits are carved and studded with whole cloves for a delicate blend of citrus and spice. Gather small holiday trims and give them new life when you make a **Christmas Red Wreath**. The items are wired together and then painted with all shades of Christmas red. Make a **Colorful Jester Stocking** using scraps of satin and bright jingle bells. Instructions for all of the projects start on page 221.

A little paint, a dusting of glitter, and purchased acrylic fruit combine to make a lovely **Wintergreen Centerpiece**. Brightly colored shells, available at crafts stores, are glued to a purchased wreath form to make a colorful **Seashell Wreath**. Use naturally-colored shells for a more subtle version of the wreath. Showcase the wreath with towels to match.

Don't forget the birds at holiday time. These **Beautiful Ice Globes** are made using balloons, water, and bird seed. As they melt, the birds enjoy the seeds. Instructions for all of the projects start on page 223.

Light up the outside of your holiday home with the magic of the season with **Beribboned Christmas Lanterns**.

Any style of lantern can become a bright addition to your outside decorating with just a little bit of trimming. Simply match the theme of the decorating to the style of the light.

For a rustic lantern choose a **Pinecone and Feather Trim.** Make a **Holiday Red Lantern** by tying a bow and securing it to the top of a white lightpost. Trim a painted lantern with a matching color of ribbon and a piece of vintage jewelry to make a **Jeweled Lantern**. Add a tiny bead garland to finish the look. Instructions for all of the projects start on page 225.

Decorating All Through the House

Create a pair of **Vintage Christmas Stockings** using a favorite retro fabric or a reproduction feedsack fabric reminiscent of the 1930s. Tiny snowflakes are painted on a purchased phone to create a **Friendly Winter Hello**. Use fine-line permanent markers to draw the little motifs.

Choose a favorite basket to hang at your front door and fill it with fresh fruit, greens, and nuts for a **Fruit Basket Welcome**. Bright and cheery fabrics are quilted together to make a favorite **Lines and Dots Stocking**. The strips are sewn together and the dots are machine-appliquéd onto the fabrics. Make a bright and shiny **Gift Bow Wreath** using purchased bows and wreath form. Instructions for all of the projects start on page 226.

W rap some extra pretty packages to decorate your bookshelves for quick holiday decorating. It is so easy to make **Christmas Package Bookends** that actually serve to hold your books in place and look like hidden Christmas gifts.

Begin by choosing your favorite books to showcase on your shelves. We chose books in the colors of Christmas—red and green—that had beautifully embellished fronts and spines. The books are held upright with a stack of packages that have been weighted. Tie pretty ribbons around the boxes to complete the bookends. Instructions for making the bookends start on page 230.

*M*ake your windows say "Merry Christmas" just like every other part of your holiday home with clever **Window Dress-Ups**. A simple purchased wreath becomes a colorful **Berry Wreath Accent** by simply pulling the fabric through the wreath. Pinecones painted a sparkling silver combine with twisted sheer ribbon to become a **Pinecone Tie Back**. The pinecones are wired to the ribbon after it is tied around the curtain. Vintage bells adorn Christmas red ribbon to make a simple **Christmas Bells Tie**. The bells are strung on the ribbon and tied around the curtain. Instructions for all of the dress-ups start on page 230.

G reet your guests with a handmade wreath of jeweled fruits and magnolia leaves. The **Traditional Welcome Wreath** can be made in the size to fit your door. Refresh a castaway vintage typewriter with fresh paint to make a **Retro Greeting** that will add an unexpected twist to your decorating.

Your family and friends will feel most welcome when they see your handiwork in a **Welcome Cross Stitch**. Use rubber stamps to decorate an old pair of ice skates—then add them as the centerpiece to a purchased wreath to create a **Frosted Ice Skate Wreath**. Simple stitches make **Homespun Felt Stockings** so easy to make. Make a set for yourself and for a quick gift. Instructions for all of the projects start on page 232.

❧ Sparkling Holiday Frames

Purchased wooden picture frames are dressed for the holidays with Christmas stickers and ultra-fine glitter.

What you need

Purchased wooden picture frames (ours have 4x6-inch openings that accommodate the antique postcards shown)
Purchased holiday stickers
Clear crafts glue
Fine white glitter

What you do

Arrange stickers on the frames as desired. Try to choose sticker sheets that have some line stickers included that connect the individual stickers. This makes for a more cohesive design. After the stickers are all in place, use your finger to rub some clear glue very lightly over the stickers and the frame. Dust lightly with the fine glitter. Allow to dry. Using old photos, prints, or copies of antique postcards, put pictures in the frames.

Paper Holly Wreath

Green papers in all shades and bright red jingle bells form this holly wreath that welcomes your holiday guests.

What you need

Tracing paper, pencil
9-inch plastic foam wreath, such as Styrofoam
Green tissue paper; scissors
Large corsage pin
Short straight pins
Various colors of green cardstock (paper should be green on both sides)

Clear strong crafts glue, such as E6000
Small red jingle bells
Tack crafts glue
Fine red glitter

What you do

Trace the holly patterns, *below,* onto tracing paper. Trace around each pattern onto the various pieces of solid and patterned green cardstock. You will need about 45 holly leaves in

Holly Leaf Patterns

various sizes. Cut out the leaves, bend slightly down the middle; set aside. Cut strips of tissue paper and wrap the wreath form until it is covered, pinning as needed to hold. Using the large corsage pin, poke a hole at the top of each leaf. Group the leaves by threes and pin to the tissue-covered wreath, arranging as desired. When the arrangement is done, gently lift the leaves and secure with glue. Glue the red jingle bells in groups between the leaves. Allow to dry. Dab a little crafts glue on the jingle bells and dust with fine red glitter. Let dry.

Merry Christmas Lampshade

The beautiful age-old art of paper punching is the technique used to create light and shadow on this festive shade. We used a star pattern and a simple "Merry Christmas" to accent our shade, but any greeting or shape will work well to bring sparkling light to your holiday room.

What you need

Tracing paper
Pencil
Purchased lampshade (we chose an ecru shade that is 3¼ inches across at the top and 11 inches across at the bottom)
Transparent tape
T-pin

What You Do

Trace the patterns, *below*, onto tracing paper. Cut around the patterns leaving about ½ inch around each pattern. Arrange the patterns on the lampshade where desired. You can use the patterns more than once, or you can make multiples of each pattern. Tape the patterns in place. Using the T-pin, start poking holes through the shade. The holes should be about ⅛ to ¼ inch apart. Continue poking holes until the pattern is completed. Remove the tracing paper.

Lampshade Punch Pattern

219

Cuff Pattern
Cut 2

Happy Holiday Stockings

Layers of long white fringe accent bright polka dot fabric to make these fun-to-hang-up stockings. Use them for Santa to fill on Christmas Eve or hang on a door knob or chair for a happy and bright decoration.

What you need

Photocopier or scanner
Pencil
Scissors
Two 10x16-inch towels (or fabric pieces) for each stocking
½ yard contrast fabric with light body or stiffness (for lining)
¼ yard white felt (for cuff)
22 inches of 3-inch-wide white fringe trim
2⅓x7-inch strip of fabric for loop

What you do

Enlarge stocking patterns, *right*, and cut out. Cut out pattern pieces from appropriate fabrics. Stitch stocking pieces with right sides together, leaving top edge open, using ¼ inch

Happy Holidays
Stocking Pattern

Enlarge 200%

Stocking Pattern
Cut 2 from fabric
Cut 2 from lining

seam. Clip curves. Turn right side out. Stitch lining pieces with right sides together, using ⅜ inch seam. Trim the seam close to stitching to reduce bulk in stocking. Turn in long edges of loop, bringing long edges to center. Fold in half and stitch close to long open edge. Insert lining inside turned stocking, keeping top straight edges even. Fold loop in half and baste to upper back edge of stocking on lining side. Stitch fringe across front cuff piece, making three even rows across. Top edge of fringe should be ½ inch to ⅝ inch from long edge. Stitch ends of cuff, right sides together.

Pin right side of cuff to wrong side of stocking. Stitch. Turn cuff to outside. Press stocking body lightly.

🌿 Candy Cane Greeting

Gather together all shapes and sizes of peppermint sticks and candy canes and arrange them in a favorite vintage basket.

What you need

Vintage or new basket
Cut pieces of fresh evergreen
Candy canes in all shapes and sizes (see Sources, page 239)
Purchased red and white beaded garland

What you do

Arrange the fresh greens in the basket. Drape the beaded garland around the edges of the basket and secure in place by tucking into the greens.

Place the candy canes in the greens, varying the sizes and shapes in the basket. Add more greens to secure the candy in place.

🌿 Citrus Pomanders

Using an unexpected tool to carve these winter fruits yields a lovely and aromatic centerpiece. Let the children place the cloves into the center of each star. Have a bowl of sliced oranges for snacking while you work together.

What you need

Fresh oranges, lemons, and limes
Pencil
Whole cloves
Linoleum cutter (available at crafts and discount stores)
Fresh evergreens
Cinnamon sticks

What you do

Choose the desired piece of fruit. With a pencil, mark a dot where you want to carve the stars on the fruit. Using the linoleum cutter and cutting away from yourself, make a star by carving an X at the dot and then making another line across the X once or twice through the middle, forming a star. Continue making stars randomly on the fruits.

Push a whole clove in the center of each star. Place several pieces of fruit in a clear glass bowl with cinnamon sticks and fresh greens. This centerpiece will stay fresh for approximately three days.

Special Tip
Fruit has always been a big part of Christmas celebrations. During the 1800s fruit was usually available only in season and locally, so if a family lived in the northern part of the country, an orange or grapefruit at Christmas time was a much appreciated gift. Use fruits as decoration in baskets, on mantels, and as gifts to rekindle this fond Christmas memory.

Christmas Red Wreath

What color says Christmas more than beautiful Christmas red? A little metallic spray paint and traditional tree tinsel combine with knickknacks and castaway trims to make this elegantly red holiday statement.

What you need

Small Christmas items, such as acrylic
  fruit, Santas, reindeer ornaments, etc.
Newspapers
Primer, such as Kilz
Red metallic spray paint
10-inch plastic foam wreath form, such as
  Styrofoam
Packages of red tinsel garland
Short straight pins; scissors
Hot-glue gun and glue sticks
¼-inch-wide red satin ribbon
1-inch red muffin cup liners
3-inch-wide red wire edge ribbon for bow

What you do

Choose the items you want to put on the wreath. Lay them on the newspaper and paint with primer. Allow to dry. Paint the items with the metallic red paint. Allow to dry. Set aside. Cut the tinsel into 3-foot lengths to make it easier to wrap the form. Starting anywhere on the back side of wreath, pin one end of the tinsel. Start wrapping the wreath until that length of tinsel is used. Add another

length and continue until the wreath is entirely wrapped. Pin the end of the tinsel on the back. Hot-glue the painted Christmas items to the tinsel. Make tiny fans by cutting a section from the muffin liners. Poke a hole in the corner and add a ribbon. Hot-glue onto wreath. Tie a bow with the wire-edge ribbons and glue to center of wreath.

Colorful Jester Stocking

Stripes of satin and bright red jingle bells combine to make this happy stocking.

What you need

Tracing paper
Pencil; scissors
Pinking shears
½ yard each of yellow and purple satin
½ yard of iron-on fleece
1 yard of red satin
Red sewing thread
4 small red jingle bells

Jester Stocking Pattern

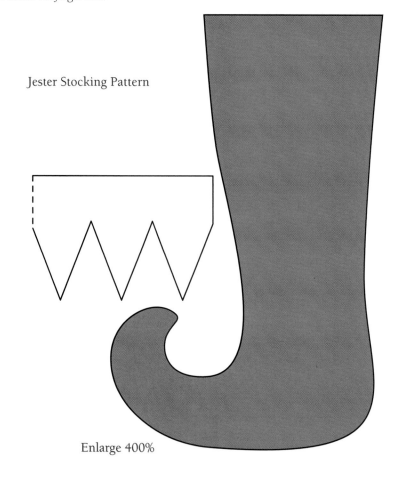

Enlarge 400%

What you do

Enlarge and trace stocking and cuff patterns, *opposite*. Cut out patterns. Cut two stocking pieces from iron-on fleece. From red satin, cut two stocking lining pieces. From red satin, cut two cuff pieces from pattern, placing side on fold, adding ¼-inch seam allowances on all other edges. Set aside.

Using pinking shears, cut yellow, purple, and red satin into strips measuring 14-inches long and varying in widths from 1 to 3 inches. In desired order, piece together enough strips to equal two pieces of pieced fabric approximately 14x21 inches each. Cut stocking front and back from pieced fabric, adding ¼-inch seam allowances to all sides.

Cut a 1x8-inch piece of red satin for hanging loop. Iron fleece onto the back of front and back stocking pieces. Sew right sides together, using ¼-inch seams and leaving top edges free. Clip curves, turn, and press. With right sides together, sew lining stocking pieces together using ¼-inch seams. Clip seams. With right sides together, fold long sides of loop together and stitch, leaving short edges free. Turn right side out and press.

Insert lining inside stocking. Pin loop at side of stocking, having cut edges even with top unfinished edges of stocking and lining, with loop extending downward. Sew cuff pieces with right sides together, leaving long top edge open. Trim across bottom of points and clip carefully into inside points before turning and pressing.

Insert cuff inside stocking with top raw edges even and side sewn edges at side seam with hanger. Sew a ⅜-inch seam around top of stocking, joining cuff to top. Overcast edges. Flip cuff over stocking to front. Handsew jingle bells to toe and cuff points.

Wintergreen Centerpiece

This elegant centerpiece, made of acrylic fruit, will last season after season dressed in wintergreen paint and a sparkle of glitter.

What you need

Small dropcloth
Purchased artificial fruits
Spray paint in forest green
Mint green fine glitter
Fresh evergreens
Pedestal dish or bowl
Purchased garland (optional)
Vintage card (optional)

What you do

Lay out the fruits on the dropcloth leaving plenty of room around each item. Lightly spray paint on one side. Allow to dry. Turn and paint the other side. Allow to dry. Spray the tops and bottoms in the same manner, allowing to dry.

Stand the fruits up on the drop cloth and lightly spray once again. While the paint is wet, carefully dust with glitter. Allow to dry.

Layer fresh or artificial greens in the pedestal dish or bowl. Arrange the painted fruits in the bowl as desired. Add a garland or vintage card to the arrangement if desired.

Seashell Wreath

Colored seashells and a bit of glue and ribbon are all it takes to make this delightful wreath to use in those hard to decorate rooms.

What you need

Purchased 9-inch flat foam wreath form, such as Styrofoam
9-inch piece of fine wire for hanger
Painted seashells (available pre-painted at crafts and discount stores) If using found shells, paint as desired with acrylic paints
Hot-glue gun and glue sticks
1 yard of 3-inch-wide wire-edge ribbon
Fresh greens

What you do

If using found shells, paint shells in desired colors. Allow to dry. Loop wire around the top of the wreath and secure in the back for hanging. Arrange painted shells on the front of the wreath form as desired, gluing over the wire. Glue small areas at a time. Hot-glue shells along the edges of the wreath as well. Allow to dry. Tie a ribbon bow and hot-glue to the top of the wreath. Add greens to back of bow.

Special Tip
Let each child have a small dish of shells. Have them hand you the treasured pieces as you glue them on the wreath. Everyone will be proud of the results.

Beautiful Ice Globes

Catching the light of the winter sun, these glistening balls of ice are filled with goodies for your favorite feathered friends.

What you need

Round balloons
Bird seed
Orange peel
Dried cranberries or other dried fruits
Funnel (optional)
Water
Freezer

What you do

Drop the bird seed, dried fruit, and orange peel into the empty balloon. Use a funnel if desired. Fill the balloon with water and tie a knot at the top. Place in the freezer turning the balloon every 20 minutes until frozen. Remove from freezer and peel off balloon. Set outside in cold weather for the birds.

❧ Beribboned Christmas Lanterns

Bring the magic of Christmas to the outside of your home with these three lovely outdoor lighting ideas.

What you need

Items to decorate outdoor lanterns such as ribbon, small garland, fresh greens, spray snow
Wire
Wire snips
Scissors

What you do

For all of the lanterns, tie the bows first and then wire the bow to attach to the lantern or post. Wire the other embellishments to the attached bows or directly to the lantern or pole, always being sure to leave enough wire at the ends to attach the bow arrangement to the lantern. Use plenty of wire and wire tightly for outdoor decorating.

If the lantern is rustic in appearance, try a **Pinecone and Feather Trim** to adorn the light. Add a printed or colored ribbon bow.

Gold-edge wide ribbon and gold jingle bells strung on smaller coordinating ribbon combine to trim the **Holiday Red Lantern**.

The **Jeweled Lantern** has a vintage brooch pinned to the bow and is finished beautifully with a string of cut, shiny blue bead garland.

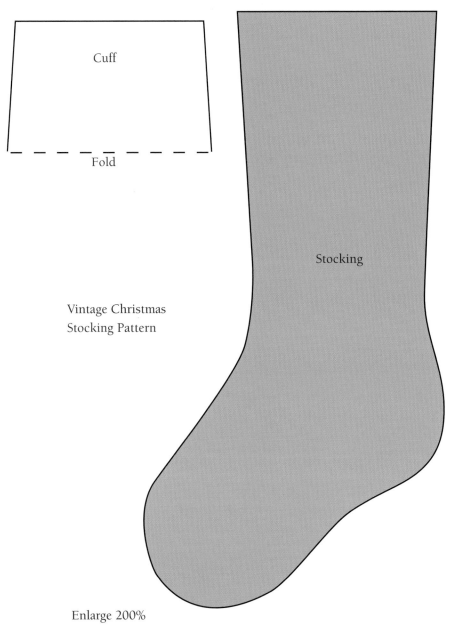

Cuff

Fold

Vintage Christmas
Stocking Pattern

Stocking

Enlarge 200%

Vintage Christmas Stockings

These Christmas stockings have a secret of their own—they were made from fabrics that had served a practical purpose before they were transformed into such charming holiday pieces.

What you need

Tracing paper
Pencil
Scissors
Fabric in desired colors (we used 1930s
  feedsack-print fabrics)
¼ yard iron-on fleece
¼ yard lining fabric
⅛ yard desired fabric for cuff
¼-inch solid color piping
Fusible webbing
Threads to match fabrics

What you do

Enlarge and trace the patterns, *above*, onto tracing paper. Cut out the patterns. With right sides of stocking fabric together, cut two stocking shapes adding ¼-inch seam allowances on all sides and ½-inch seam allowance at the top. Cut two pieces of iron-on fleece the same size. Cut two lining pieces without adding ¼-inch seam allowances. For loop, cut a 2x6-inch piece of fabric.

Iron fleece to the wrong side of each stocking. Baste piping to edge of stocking

front. Sew stocking pieces together, right sides together being careful not to catch piping in the seam. Clip curves; turn right side out. Press. Stitch lining together with right sides together using a ¼-inch seam. Clip curves. Turn, insert lining inside stocking. Baste across top of lining and stocking ½ inch from stocking top.

For loop, fold long edges of fabric into the middle and over in half again to make a ½x6-inch piece. Stitch close to fold. Fold in half with top raw edges even. Place loop inside lining of stocking and baste to top edge of stocking. For small stocking cuff, fold cuff fabric in half right sides together; place cuff pattern on fold as indicated on pattern. Cut out 2 cuff pieces leaving ¼-inch seam allowances at cuff sides and ½-inch seam allowance at top. From pattern, cut one fleece cuff piece without adding seam allowances. Cut along fold line making two pieces. Iron fleece to back of each cuff fabric, covering only half of each cuff. Machine or hand quilt the cuff, if desired. Open up cuff and with right sides together, stitch the sides of the cuff with ¼-inch seams. Fold cuff in half to form a ring, Put cuff inside stocking, with top raw edges even and right side of cuff facing lining. Stitch top together with ½-inch seam. Flip cuff to outside over stocking. Press.

❦ Friendly Winter Hello

Send those holiday greetings by telephone this year, and this oh-so-pretty snowflake-covered phone will put you in the holiday spirit. We've decorated this purchased telephone with delicate snowflakes using a fine-line paint marker. We've given some patterns for you to follow, but remember, no two snowflakes are ever alike!

What you need

Purchased telephone (we chose black in a classic style, but choose a phone that suits your holiday decor)
White chalk
Fine-line permanent paint markers in gold and white or desired colors

What you do

Be sure that the phone is clean and dry. With a piece of white chalk, mark a dot where you want to place your snowflakes. You can vary the size of the snowflakes, and group some if you wish.

Using the fine-line permanent marker and the patterns, *below,* as inspiration, draw the snowflakes on the telephone. Place the snowflakes on all areas of the phone varying the size and color. Wait for each area to dry before proceeding to another area.

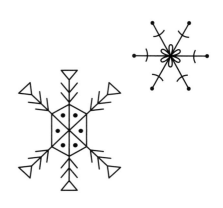

Snowflake Patterns

Lines and Dots Stocking

Santa will love to fill this happy quilted stocking constructed in no time with strip piecing. The playful circles are added with machine appliqué.

What you need

Tracing paper
Pencil
Scissors
¼ yard each red, green, purple, and yellow cotton fabrics
¼ yard striped cotton fabric for lining
Matching threads
¼ yard thin quilt batting
Small pieces polyfil or cotton balls
Fusible webbing
20x20-inch square of thin cotton batting

What you do

Enlarge and trace the stocking pattern, *opposite*. Dots are full-size. Cut two stocking pattern pieces from lining fabric. Set aside. Cut 18-inch long strips of solid fabrics varying widths ranging from 1-2 ½ inches wide. Piece together solid fabrics to make a 18x24-inch piece of fabric. Cut two stocking patterns from this pieced fabric. Cut two stocking patterns from batting and baste to both stocking pieces.

For circle embellishments

Trace circle patterns onto fusible webbing. Iron onto back of striped and yellow fabrics. Cut out circles along lines. Arrange as desired on striped pieced stocking pieces, overlapping some circles and leaving others separate.

Iron down all yellow circle shapes and buttonhole stitch around edges using matching thread. Place striped dots where desired. Before ironing striped dots to stocking, insert a small balled up piece of polyfil or piece of cotton ball underneath the striped circle shapes to give them more dimension. Lightly

iron around outside edges. Buttonhole stitch around outside edges.

With right sides together, sew stocking pieces together using ¼-inch seam allowance. Clip curves, turn and press lightly. With right sides together, sew lining pieces together. Clip curves. Iron top edges of stocking ½ inch to the inside and iron top edge of lining ½ inch to the outside. Insert lining inside the stocking. Make a hanging loop by cutting a 2x9-inch piece of striped fabric. With right sides together, stitch long edges together using a ¼-inch seam. Turn right side out and press. Insert loop at top right side of stocking between outside and lining fabrics. Baste together close to top folds. Stitch lining and stocking together by stitching close to top fold, also stitching through loop at side edge.

❦ Fruit Basket Welcome

What could be easier than hanging a fresh basket of fruit at your front door to greet your holiday guests.

What you need

Wicker basket with one flat side (available at crafts and discount stores)
Fresh fruit and nuts
Fresh greens
Red ribbon

What you do

Weave the ribbon through the wicker basket and tie a bow in the front. Hang the basket on the inside of an outdoor walkway or doorway being sure that the nails or hanger will accommodate heavy fruits. Fill the basket with greens, a variety of fruits, and nuts. In cool climates the basket of fruit will keep for a week or more.

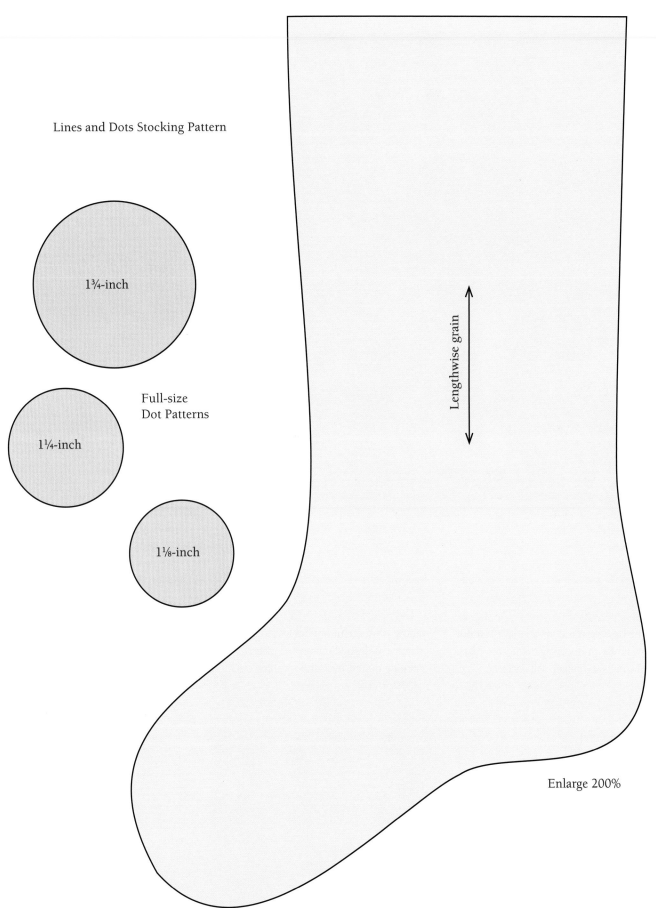

Lines and Dots Stocking Pattern

1¾-inch

Full-size
Dot Patterns

1¼-inch

1⅛-inch

Lengthwise grain

Enlarge 200%

❧ Christmas Package Bookends

They may just look like pretty packages, but these presents serve a purpose. Make a set for your holiday decorating and make an extra set for a special book-lovers gift.

❧ Gift Bow Wreath

Pretty metallic bows, so available and affordable at discount and dollar stores, line up to become a sparkling wreath just in time for Christmas. Use all the colors of Christmas, or choose bows in the palette of colors that suits your holiday color scheme.

What you need

Purchased metallic bows in a variety of sizes and shapes (from discount store)
12-inch flat plastic foam wreath, such as Styrofoam
Glue suitable for plastic
Straight pins

What you do

Lay out the bow to plan the desired arrangement on the wreath, looking at color and size of bows. Mix and match the bows in size and color for interest.

One at a time and working only on one area at a time, glue the bows to the plastic foam. Use a straight pin if necessary to hold the bows in place until the glue is dry.

Allow the wreath to dry completely and then remove the pins.

What you need

Small gift boxes
Tiny rocks or fish gravel
Transparent tape
Wrapping paper and ribbon to match vintage books
Purchased bottlebrush tree
Tacky crafts glue

What you do

Fill each of the packages with the tiny rocks or fish gravel. Tape the boxes closed. Wrap the packages with wrapping paper and ribbons to coordinate with the books to be used. (We used red and green vintage books.) Stack and glue the boxes together forming the bookends. Glue a small bottlebrush tree to the top of the box if desired.

Place the pieces on either side of the books forming the bookends.

🎄 Window Dress Ups

Try unexpected holiday trims to dress up your curtains or drapes for Christmas.

**What you need for
the Berry Wreath Accent**
Purchased berry wreath
Fresh greens; fine wire; wire cutter

**What you do for
the Berry Wreath Accent**
Wire the greens to the wreath. Pull the curtain through the wreath and arrange as desired.

**What you need for
the Pinecone Tie Back**
Pinecones and nuts painted silver
Drill with small drill bit
Fine wire; wire-edge silver ribbon

**What you do for
the Pinecone Tie Back**
Drill the nuts to make a hole large enough for the wire to go through. Wire the pinecones and the nuts to the ribbon placing items about 5 inches apart. Twist the ribbon between the pinecones and nuts and wrap around curtain.

**What you need for
the Christmas Bells Tie**
Sheer red ribbon
Bells in desired colors

**What you do for
the Christmas Bells Tie**
Thread the bells onto the ribbon and tie around the curtain.

Traditional Welcome Wreath

Traditional fruit motifs have served as a sign of holiday welcomes for generations. The range of hues and shapes that the fruit offers yields wonderful combinations of texture and color. This showy beaded fruit wreath combines the glorious colors of nature yet is so easy to make.

What you need

12-inch plastic foam wreath, such as
   Styrofoam, with flat edges
About 30 artificial magnolia leaves
Hot-glue gun and hot-glue sticks
Purchased beaded fruit with plastic foam
   core (available at crafts and discount
   stores), (we chose peaches, red and green
   apples, oranges, and pears)
Band saw
Note: *If you don't have a band saw, take
   the fruit to your hardware or home center
   and ask them to cut the artificial fruit for
   you. They may charge a minimal fee.*
Protective goggles
Thin wire for hanging

What you do

Arrange the leaves on the wreath. Overlap the leaves to cover all of the foam wreath. Hot-glue in place overlapping the leaves as you glue.

   Cut the fruit in half using a band saw. Most beaded fruit have a plastic core and are fairly easy to cut. Wear protective goggles because the tiny beads can fly off when cutting. Any artificial fruit will work, even if it is not beaded. Simply cut the fruit in half.

   Arrange the fruit over the leaves. Hot-glue in place. Make a loop from the wire and attach at the back/top of the wreath for hanging.

Retro Greeting

A vintage typewriter finds a clever place in your decorating scheme with a fresh coat of paint and a handwritten message from Santa himself. Simply spray paint the typewriter red and then hand paint the keys.

What you need

Old typewriter
Red spray paint
Gold paint suitable for metal
Small paintbrushes
6x8-inch piece of gold or patterned paper
Black fine-line marker

What you do

Spray-paint the typewriter red. The paint will overspray onto the keys. Let dry. With a small brush, paint the keys and other small areas gold. Let dry. Write a message on the paper with the marker and put in the typewriter.

Welcome Cross Stitch

A simple yet always-appropriate message is carefully planned out on this colorful Christmas cross-stitch.

What you need

*12x6-inch piece of 16-count white
 Aida cloth
Cotton embroidery floss in colors
 listed in key
Kreinik gold #8 braid
Needle; embroidery hoop
Three gold star buttons with holes
3x10½-inch piece of matboard
2 small jingle bells
¼ yard of fleece
Thick white crafts glue
3x10½-inch piece of white felt
4-inch piece of ⅛ inch dowel
1 yard of fine gold braid
2 star buttons with holes in the sides
¼ yard of thin red ribbon*

What you do

Find center of the chart and the center of the fabric; begin stitching there. Use two plies of floss for all cross-stitches. Work the backstitches using one ply of floss or braid. Press piece on back side. Sew star buttons with holes in front at X's near M. Sew small jingle bell at x near W.

To mount, cut the end of the matboard to a point. Lay stitchery over board and trim 1 inch all around. Cut fleece and felt to fit board and glue fleece to board front. Wrap stitchery around fleece and board and glue on back securing dowel at the top under stitchery. Glue felt to back.

Glue braiding around edge. Tie ribbon at corners of dowel and glue star buttons, with holes in sides, to ends. Sew jingle bell to the bottom point.

Anchor		DMC	
002	•	000	White
9046	♥	321	Christmas red
297	–	444	Lemon
239	O	702	Christmas green
132	⊞	797	Royal blue

BACKSTITCH (1X)

381	/	938	Coffee brown – leaf veins in letter "O"
	/	002	Kreinik Gold #8 braid – all other stitches

Stitch count: *155 high x 40 wide*
Finished design sizes:
*14-count fabric– 11 x 2⅞ inches
16-count fabric– 9⅝ x 2½ inches
18-count fabric– 8⅝ x 2¼ inches*

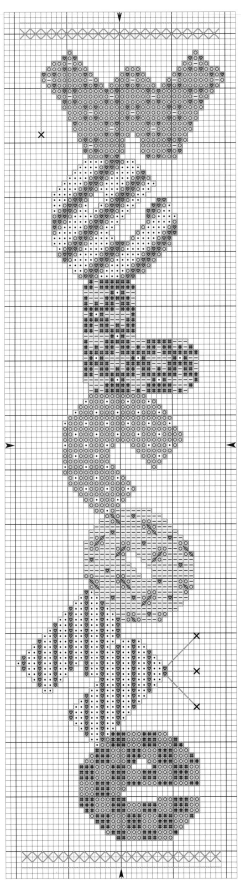

 **Frosted Ice Skate Wreath**

A pair of white ice skates become the center of attention when they are rubber-stamped with a purchased snowflake stamp and hung in the middle of a pretty green wreath. Add some jingle bells to create a happy sound.

What you need

White ice skates in a small size
Snowflake-motif rubber stamp
Red permanent ink stamp pad
Purchased artificial or real green 24-inch wreath
24-gauge wire
Wire snips
Scissors
White garland
Red berry pokes
Red jingle bells
Purchased flat snowflake ornaments
1 yard of 2-inch-wide polka dot ribbon

What you do

Be sure the skates are clean and dry. Lay each skate on a flat surface. Use the rubber stamp and the stamp pad to stamp snowflakes on the skates. Stamp one side at a time, drying one side before starting on another. Set aside to dry completely. Wrap the wreath with the white garland and secure with a little piece of wire. Wire in the berry pokes and flat snowflake ornaments. Wire the skates so they hang in the middle of the wreath. Wire the jingle bells at the top of the wreath. Tie the ribbon into a bow and wire to the top of the wreath. Add a wire hanger to the back of the wreath.

Homespun Felt Stockings

Felt comes in all colors and textures, and even with its own eyelet trim. First, make a simple stocking and trim it with a running stitch. Then finish it with a lovely cuff using purchased eyelet trim.

What you need

Photocopier or scanner
Pencil
Scissors
13-inch piece of felt for each stocking
7-inch strip of purchased eyelet felt for cuffs
⅜x6-inch strip of felt for loop
Embroidery floss

What you do

Enlarge stocking pattern, *right*, and cut out. Cut patterns from appropriate fabrics, cutting front and back from felt and cuff from eyelet fabric, making sure that the eyelet design is at the bottom of the cuff pattern. Mark toe and heal stitching lines. Using the running stitch, stitch lines on stocking fronts using 6 strands of embroidery floss. For running stitch diagram, *see page 149.*

Sew stocking pieces with right sides together, using ¼ inch seam, leaving top straight edge open. Clip curves.

Fold loop in half and baste to upper back edge of stocking on lining side.

Stitch short ends of cuff, right sides together. Pin right side of cuff to wrong side of stocking. Stitch with ¼ inch seam. Turn cuff to outside, turning stocking right side out. Press lightly.

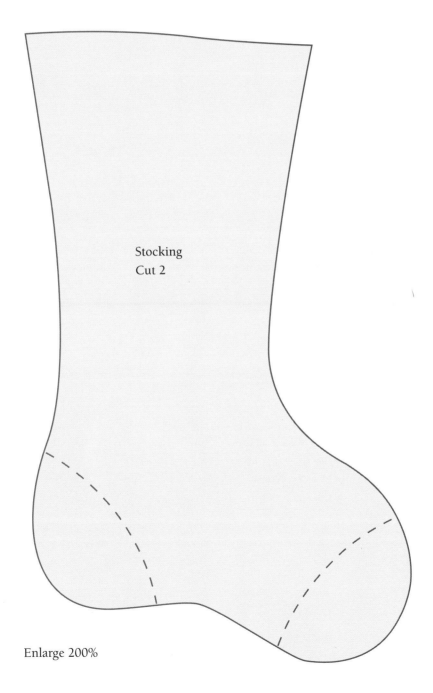

Cuff
Cut 2

Stocking
Cut 2

Homespun Felt
Stocking Pattern

Enlarge 200%

Candles 101 Add sparkle to your holiday with candles of all kinds.

Novelty Candles
These candles come in every possible shape and size. Often the shapes depict trees, vegetables, flowers, or other realistic forms.

Pillar Candles
Pillars are chunky round candles that vary in height. Sometimes they have more than one wick if the candle is very large.

Tapers
Long and thin and one of the most common of all candles, tapers used to be handmade by dipping a wick in wax and letting it hang to dry.

Ball Candles
Spheres of wax with a simple wick in the middle make ball candles.

Glass Surround Candles
Some candles are poured directly into a glass container. These candles can be lit without another holder to catch the melted wax.

Floating Candles
Designed to be able to float in water while they are lit, floating candles come in all shapes.

Tea Lights
These very small candles are poured into a metal liner and are usually used in glass holders. The liner keeps the wax from spilling into the container.

Votives
Small candles that are cylindrical in shape make up one of the most common candle types.

More Ideas

Have a favorite friend come over for hot cider and work together decorating your home. Then go to her home and do the same. Think of all the fun visiting (and holiday planning) you can do while you work!

For a school room decoration for your child's teacher, get a class picture from each student. Trim and glue the pictures to a purchased wreath form and add a bow.

Embellish an artificial green wreath by hot-gluing favorite board game pieces such as checkers, chess pieces, or dice to the wreath. Add a bow and hang in the game room.

Top a purchased evergreen wreath with a bow tied from a vintage handkerchief. Search antiques stores or flea markets to find a handkerchief with Christmas motifs or in the colors of Christmas.

Overlap and glue colorful Christmas diecuts from the scrapbook store to a purchased wreath form to make a quick wreath.

Holiday fabrics can add a splash of color to your holiday decorating when turned into no-sew table runners, napkins, tree skirts, and torn-fabric bows.

For kitchen fun, place holiday cookie cutters in a large, clear-glass jar tied with a ribbon, or display clear red cookie cutters in the window.

Replace throw rugs with holiday-themed ones. You can find a large selection at home and discount stores.

Spray-paint large terra-cotta pots bright gold and fill with pinecones and the tops of real evergreens for festive walkway decorations.

Use groupings of small, colorful Christmas ornaments as tiebacks on curtains. Tie three or more ornaments together with holiday ribbon or colored wire and tie in the center of the curtain.

Use clippings of real evergreen everywhere. Tuck snips of this aromatic greenery above doorways, in baskets, on window sills, and in bookcases. You'll enjoy the wonderful scent of the season wherever you go.

With narrow ribbons, tie holiday cookies and cookie cutters to evergreen swags and hang them on your banister to make your stairway look sweet.

Paint a purchased pine cone wreath with metallic green spray paint for a stunningly simple and very sparkling holiday wreath.

Choose pictures of you and your friends or family members and frame them in a purchased frame for a quick qift. The gift will mean even more with a picture of you together in it.

Index

Sources

Adhesives/Tapes
Quick Grip all-purpose
  permanent adhesive
Quick Grip Beacon Adhesives
125 MacQuesten Parkway
South
Mount Vernon, NY 10550
914-699-3400
www.beaconcreates.com

ArtAccentz
Provo Craft
Spanish Fork, Utah 84660
www.provocraft.com

Art Supplies
American Craft
www.americancrafts.com

Hobby Lobby
www.hobbylobby.com

Michaels Arts & Crafts
www.michaels.com
1-800-michaels

Mod Podge
www.plaidonline.com

QuicKutz
www.quickutz.com

Beading Supplies
Michael Arts & Crafts
www.michaels.com
1-800-michaels

Candy
Hammond's Candies
www. hammondscandies.com

Cookie Cutters, Cookie and Cake Decorating Supplies
Maid of Scandinavia by
Sweet Celebrations
1-800-328-6722
www.sweetc.com

Fabric Stabilizer/Pellon
6932 SW Macadam Ave.,
Suite A
Portland, Oregon 97219
1-866-333-4463
www.createforless.com

Glitter
The Art Institute
www.artglitter.com

Greeting Card Blanks/ Envelopes
Pure Paper
Windsor Heights, IA 50311
515-255-3533
www.pure-paper.com

Peppermint Chips
Andes Peppermint Crunch
www.tootsie.com

Ribbon
www.craftopia.com
www.hancockfabrics.com
www.joannfabrics.com
www.jordanpapercrafts.com
www.mayarts.com
www.midoriribbon.com
www.mjtrim.com
www.papermart.com
www.offray.com
www.ribbonlady.com
www.ribbonshop.com

Scrapbook Papers
Holiday Paper Squares
Brave Ink Press
515-964-1777
www.braveink.com

Stickers
EK Success
P.O. Box 1141
Clifton, NJ 07014-1141
1-800-524-1349
www.eksuccess.com

Crystal Stickers
www.markrichardsusa.com

Michaels Arts & Crafts
www.michaels.com
1-800-michaels

Wire
Michaels Arts & Crafts
www.michaels.com
1-800-michaels

Wood Letters
Provo Crafts
Spanish Fork, Utah 84660
www.provocraft.com

Wreaths
Target
100 Target Brands, Inc.
www.target.com

Michaels Arts & Crafts
www.michaels.com
1-800-michaels

Yarns
Lily Cotton
100 Sonwil Drive
Buffalo, NY 14225
PHONE 1-800-265-2684
FAX 1-888-571-6229

Also from Brave Ink Press

If you liked this book, look for other books from Brave Ink Press.

- Simply Christmas
- Christmas–Make it Sparkle
- Beautiful Christmas
- An Ornament a Day
- College Kids Cook
- Cool Crafts to Make even if you don't have a creative bone in your body!
- Easy Decorating Ideas even if you don't have a creative bone in your body!
- Christmas Together
- Christmas Happy and Bright
- The Little Book of Christmas Alphabets
- Merry Christmas Ideas

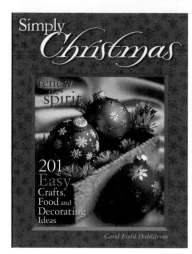

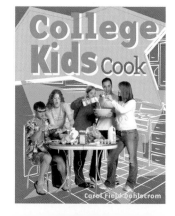

To order books, visit us at www.braveink.com or call 515-964-1777.